PERCEPTION
OF REALITY

AN EXPLORATION OF CONSCIOUSNESS

GREGORY CALISE

© Copyright 2003 Gregory Calise. All rights reserved.

No part of this publication may be reproduced, stored in a retrieval system, or transmitted, in any form or by any means, electronic, mechanical, photocopying, recording, or otherwise, without the written prior permission of the author.

Printed in Victoria, Canada

National Library of Canada Cataloguing in Publication

Calise, Gregory, 1953-
    Perceptions of reality : an exploration of consciousness / Gregory Calise.

ISBN 1-55395-661-3
    I. Title.

B105.C477C34 2003   158.1   C2003-900284-5

TRAFFORD

This book was published *on-demand* **in cooperation with Trafford Publishing.**
On-demand publishing is a unique process and service of making a book available for retail sale to the public taking advantage of on-demand manufacturing and Internet marketing.
On-demand publishing includes promotions, retail sales, manufacturing, order fulfilment, accounting and collecting royalties on behalf of the author.

Suite 6E, 2333 Government St., Victoria, B.C. V8T 4P4, CANADA
Phone   250-383-6864   Toll-free   1-888-232-4444 (Canada & US)
Fax   250-383-6804   E-mail   sales@trafford.com
Web site   www.trafford.com   TRAFFORD PUBLISHING IS A DIVISION OF TRAFFORD HOLDINGS LTD.
Trafford Catalogue #03-0024   www.trafford.com/robots/03-0024.html

10   9   8   7   6   5   4   3   2   1

This book is dedicated to the great *rishi*
Bhaktivinode Thakur,
For his most profound revelations
of the absolute reality.

CONTENTS

INTRODUCTION 1
Solving the Riddle

1. PERCEPTIONS OF KNOWLEDGE 7
Sense perception - 7
Objective vs. subjective knowledge - 10
Revelation - 11
The different religions - 12
The basic premises - 16

2. CHANGING PERSPECTIVES 19
Our binary system of opposites - 19
Polarities and perspective - 20
Perspective, conception and movement - 22
Perspective and time - 23
The blind men and the elephant - 24
Prelude to perceptions - 26

3. PERCEPTIONS OF GOD 29
So many gods - 29
God is simultaneously
   personal and impersonal - 31

The threefold manifestation
   of divine potency -   32
All opposites are reconciled in the absolute -   34
God is all powerful -   35
Other attributes of godhead -   36
Our limited conceptions of godhead -   37
The demigods -   39

4. WHO AM I? 41
The seer and the seen -   41
Characteristics of the soul -   42
The sojourn of the soul -   43

5. ETERNAL AND CAUSAL NATURE 47

6. WHAT IS THE WORLD ? 51
The framework of the cosmos -   51
The seven Hermetic principles of creation -   56
Time -   57
The material cosmos is a perverted
   reflection of the spiritual cosmos -   58
Our perceptions of the world -   60

7. THE SUBCONSCIOUS WORLD 63

8. WHAT IS THE PATH? 69
The soul's itinerary -   69
Free will or destiny? -   70
Educational system as analogy -   73

Understanding one's nature -   74
Celibacy? -   75
False austerity -   77
Sense control -   77
Desire -   79
The only one way syndrome -   80
The divisions of spiritual paths -   81
Universal actions and qualities -   82
Finding one's own path -   83

9. THE GREAT SECRETS OF PERCEPTION 85
The world is perfect -   86
The external world is a
   reflection of the internal world -   90
The world is as we perceive it to be -   92
The physics of perception -   96
The power of thought and emotion -   102
The power of gratitude -   105

ABOUT THE AUTHOR 111

PERCEPTIONS OF REALITY

Introduction

Solving the Riddle

Since time immemorial, humankind has been asking these three profound questions: "Who am I?" "From where have I come?" "What is this place?" The amazing thing is that throughout the ages, these questions have been answered many times by the various prophets and sages; albeit each in their own unique way. So, if the questions have already been answered, then why do we keep asking these same questions? Science and physics are dissecting reality to understand these questions. Psychology is exploring the depths of consciousness, and religion and philosophy are searching for the same answers.

Is it because the answers of the prophets and sages are incorrect? Or maybe they are incomplete. Maybe there isn't enough scientific knowledge to satisfy us, or maybe we just don't believe them. Then again, could it be that we just can't understand them? Why are we having such a problem to understand these three basic questions of life? After thousands of years of searching, we still are not certain of the answers.

The problem in finding the answers to these questions has always

PERCEPTIONS OF REALITY

been in our perception. Our perception of reality is dependent upon our perspective. From our present perspective in physical time and space, we cannot see beyond the apparent. We cannot see what is behind this physical reality. In fact, modern science denies that there is anything beyond our immediate physical world. Therefore they bind us to their limited reality by convincing us that anything beyond our physical reality is fantasy. With this level of perception, it is impossible to answer these three questions of life.

The great sages and prophets, due to their spiritual consciousness, have viewed the reality from a different perspective than the rest of us. Their perceptions of the truth have always been of a different nature than the common people. They can see beyond the apparent into the depths of reality. We cannot grasp their perceptions, because we refuse to let go of our present limited perspective. Therefore, when they answer the questions, we cannot quite grasp their meanings.

It is like trying to understand the taste of honey, without ever tasting it before. Someone can describe it to us, show it to us, we can even lick the outside of the jar. But until we actually taste it, we will never really know what it actually tastes like. When the prophets explain the absolute to us, it is like trying to explain color to someone who has been blind his entire life. We might be able to understand the concept, but we just can't quite grasp the actual truth.

We are trying to understand that which is beyond our normal abilities; but, in actuality, we do have within us the ability to understand these truths. The key to unlock our latent potential for understanding our world and the absolute is in our ability to change our perceptions. We can change our perceptions by changing our perspective. When we reach this higher perspective, our perceptions will change.

The great sages and prophets have been able to reach these higher perspectives and access these heightened abilities to perceive the reality. By utilizing certain principles, they have opened their hearts and accessed the abstract mind, with its heightened mental functions. Their thought processes are then of a different nature than the rest of us.

By accessing the abstract mind, they are then able to see reality from a higher perspective. Not only that, but they are also viewing reality in a different direction. They are looking up towards the heavens, towards the light. We, on the other hand, are looking down towards the earth. When one looks in the opposite direction, the view is obviously different. Even when the prophets look down towards the earth, their perceptions are of a different nature than ours. They are viewing from a higher vantage point, so they can see the whole picture.

In our present state of existence, we are viewing only a small sector of time and space. The prophets, on the other hand, are viewing reality from a higher perspective, so they can see a larger picture of life. They can see the connections and circumstances that are outside of our purview. Their horizons of perception are beyond our tiny limits, so they can see what is behind the apparent. Because of this, when the prophets and sages speak to us, they are speaking from a position that includes a larger picture; one that we cannot see.

So, in reality, the questions have already been answered, but we cannot comprehend them. Therefore, we keep asking the same questions, and we never quite understand the answers. This is because we have been looking from a lower vantage point, in the wrong place and in the wrong direction. If you are searching for light, you cannot find it in darkness. As long as we insist on keeping our present perspective of reality, we will never be able to answer these three basic questions of our existence.

The solution to this dilemma is locked within our consciousness. We need only to change our perspective to understand that which has been evident all along. When we do this, our perceptions automatically change as well, as our horizons of consciousness expand.

But how do we change our perspective? I am hoping that with this small book, you will be able to grasp the principles necessary to accomplish this. When this happens, your lives will change dramatically, because not only will you be able to answer these three questions, but many of the questions of humanity.

To attain a higher perspective, we must let go of the one that we are now holding onto. This is a scary proposition, because our present perspective is also our foundation that we use to understand reality. This requires a leap of faith. It takes faith in a higher principle, that we will be safe by taking such a leap. I can honestly tell you that you will be safe. So many people in the past have taken this leap, and they have landed safely on the other side. Once you reach the other shore of consciousness, you will be able to understand the world, yourself and the truth.

The perspective that we must leave behind is based upon our past conditioning. It is this past conditioning that creates our belief structure that binds us to our present perspective of reality. It is a false foundation, that we believe will protect us; but because it is based upon illusion, it cannot. In reality, it holds us in a type of bondage. When we let go of our past, and trust in the present moment, we will be able to reach new heights of consciousness. Our hearts will open with gratitude, and we will be able to access the abstract mind.

By accessing the abstract mind, the right and left hemispheres of the brain work in unison. This is the mind of the genius, where solutions are found. It is also the doorway to revelation, where divine truth is found. By accessing this doorway to higher consciousness, we can perceive reality in a new light, allowing access for the divine to descend into the world.

It is perception that is the key. The world becomes as we perceive it to be. Due to our past conditioning, we view the world according to

PERCEPTIONS OF REALITY

our belief structures. The world then interfaces with our belief structure and creates a world that resonates to our beliefs. If we believe the world to be a certain way, it manifests according to our beliefs. By changing our belief structures, we will change our perspective, which changes our perceptions. We can then become free from the shackles of illusion, and we will see reality from a different level of consciousness.

When this happens, you will realize that the truth was there, in front of you, all along. This awakening is like being in a dark room and then opening a door to let the light in. Everything becomes more obvious in the light, and you will have wondered how you lived without it.

PERCEPTIONS OF REALITY

PERCEPTIONS OF REALITY

1. Perceptions of Knowledge
Sense Perception

We acquire knowledge of the world through our five senses: sight, hearing, touch, taste and smell. When the sense organs come into contact with the objects of the senses, the information is transmitted to the mind. Our mind then sorts the knowledge, analyzes it, categorizes it, judges it and stores it as memory. We try to understand the knowledge or event by utilizing the mental faculties to come to some conclusion.

The way we analyze anything new, such as an event or knowledge, is that we immediately relate it to our past knowledge, events and experiences that are similar. We compare the new knowledge with the past knowledge in our memory, which we use as a foundation, in an attempt to understand our reality. In this way our past knowledge and events, and the emotions that are connected to them, are always affecting our present experiences, and unfortunately they also distort the new knowledge. Our past knowledge, events and experiences are like colored lenses that are constantly tinting our present life.

Depending on one's past knowledge, a person will view the world from a unique perspective. This in turn distorts the perception. Our past knowledge and experiences, and the emotions that are connected

PERCEPTIONS OF REALITY

to them, form our conditioning and our personal belief structure, which create our perspective, from which we perceive our reality. The conditioning of an individual is formed by family, friends, tribe, nationalism, race, religion, society, culture, genetics, teachers, vocation, politics, science, education, advertising, and personal experiences.

Because of this distortion of perception, every individual views the world in his own unique way. Depending on the individual's previous experiences, and how he has processed them, the present perceptions will be affected. Any new knowledge that one acquires will be overlaid by these previous factors.

Our past conditioning and belief structures also create our specific attitudes in life. An attitude is defined as a state of mind. In psychology, the normal mental function is divided into three divisions of attitudes. They are child, parent and adult. Each of these divisions of attitudes have positive and negative attributes. The child attitude is natural, adaptive, rebellious and the "little know it all." The parent attitude is nurturing, protecting, critical and punishing. The adult attitude is logical, rational, and the decision maker. We alternate between these three attitude states, sometimes from second to second.

Each of our attitudes are created from our past conditioning and beliefs, especially from childhood. These attitudes also help define our perspective from which we perceive reality. Our perceptions in life are then dependent on our past knowledge and conditioning, which create certain attitudes, or states of mind. These create our perspective from which we perceive the world.

Now if each person has his own unique perception of the same world, there will occur differences in opinions concerning knowledge, events and circumstances. We experience this every day in our lives, as people are constantly disagreeing on even trivial issues.

This problem is very evident in the fields of philosophy and religion. These subjects are very esoteric and difficult to prove, so it

PERCEPTIONS OF REALITY

seems likely that we should find so many differing opinions. If you ask different individuals to read the same philosophical treatise, they will each perceive it according to their past conditioning. If you were to read the different commentaries from different philosophers on the same philosophical treatise, you would see many differences and many similarities, depending upon the perceptions of the commentators.

Many times the purports will even be in opposition to each other. We see this in every religion. Depending upon the different understandings (perceptions) of philosophers, different denominations spring up. Even within the same denominations, individuals can come to completely opposite conclusions. For example, Christ taught peace and brotherly love, yet the Inquisition occurred by the order of the Church, based on Christ's teachings.

How can we understand that completely opposite conclusions can come from the same philosophy? If we see that each individual has a unique conditioning and a unique perception of reality, then it would only be natural that each person's understanding of truth is also unique.

Most truths in our world are relative, as we live in a relative world of opposites, or duality. What constitutes our perception in a relative world is our perspective. Our perspective is dictated by our position in relation to the object being observed. Our past conditioning and belief structure affect our position.

The definition of relative is that which is not absolute and independent; a thing having a relation to or connection with or necessary dependent on another thing. This world, by nature, is relative. It is a world of relationship and duality and depending upon our perspective, our perception of it is relative. What I may perceive as bad, you may perceive as good; what I may perceive as cold, you may perceive as warm; what I may perceive as success, you may perceive as failure.

PERCEPTIONS OF REALITY

Each person perceives the world in a relative way according to his past conditioning.

Objective vs. Subjective Knowledge

Objective means having reality independent of mind; relating to or being an object, phenomenon, or condition in the realm of sensible experience independent of individual thought and perceptible by all observers.

Subjective means relating to or determined by the mind as the subject of experience; characteristic of or belonging to reality as perceived rather than as independent from mind; relating to or being experience or knowledge as conditioned by personal mental characteristics or states.

Most of what we consider as objective knowledge is in fact only subjective. It is either one person's or a group of people's perception of an objective fact. Most of our knowledge of science, chemistry, medicine, physics, astronomy, archeology, anthropology, sociology, religion and philosophy are all only our subjective analysis and perception of objective reality. Our world and the entire universe are objective realities, but our perceptions of them are only subjective. Just because a certain group of people perceive a reality in the same way does not mean that their perceptions are true. The amazing thing is that what is actually our subjective perception of reality is taught as objective knowledge. Many times they are only theories. Take for example evolution: It is taught as an objective fact, when in fact it is only a theory. Evolution has never been proven scientifically.

Let's look at another example of how our perceptions are considered as objective fact. Let's look at medicine: An allopathic doctor views the body in one way; a doctor of Chinese medicine will view it in another way; a holistic doctor will view it in yet another way; a physicist in another; and a shaman in still another way.

If we look at all of the subjects of knowledge above (science, medicine, astronomy, etc.), we see that they are constantly changing. For example, a little over 500 years ago we thought the earth was flat. At the time it was considered an objective fact. That perception has changed. We used to think that the earth was the center of the solar system. That has also changed. Much of what we thought was factual in every area of knowledge has changed, especially in the last century.

In modern physics, we are learning that the world isn't what it seems to be at all, but what it seems to be is only a semblance or projection of the underlying reality. According to physics, the world is actually made up of frequencies of energy, and our sense organs and brain convert and organize these frequencies into information that we can process and form as reality. According to the famous physicist David Bohm and others, this entire universe is actually a hologram.

As we progress in our understanding of reality by research and exploration, our foundations and beliefs are shifting so quickly that our concept of reality is becoming ever more evasive. What convictions we may have of a certain subject may be shattered instantaneously, leaving us with little choice but to create new foundations on which to rest our new convictions. Eventually we will reach a point of consciousness where all of our previous convictions will be shattered, creating a new form of consciousness in which to perceive reality.

Revelation

There is another type of knowledge which is not received through our senses. This knowledge is revelation and inspiration. Revelation is an act of revealing or communicating divine truth. Whereas the knowledge of the world, which is received via the senses, is relative, revelation, on the other hand, is absolute. Absolute means free from imperfection, being self-sufficient and free of external relationships. Revelations are completely different from relative knowledge, as they are absolute objective reality. They originate from an absolute realm of consciousness and descend into our relative realm of consciousness through the abstract mind. The abstract mind is the mental function that links the right and left hemispheres of the brain.

Yet even divine revelations may be prone to misconceptions and misperceptions by our normal mental functions, and are therefore sometimes still subjective. When we receive visions of spiritual knowledge or visions of gods and saints, our normal, non-abstract mind will try to assimilate the knowledge in the same way it does with sensory knowledge. It will refer to past memories to try to understand the revelation; to see how it fits into one's belief system. One may even try to apply logic and reasoning to the revelation. Because of this, the revelation, which is an absolute objective reality, may become subject to our subjective perception. If one's heart and mind are pure, then the revelation will not be affected or distorted by these mental processes.

The Different Religions

We will now look at how and why so many different religions have manifested upon the earth. A universal physical and metaphysical law of the universe is that everything material is temporary. This also holds true for religious doctrines. The purpose of religion is eternal; to cultivate a proper relationship between the spirit soul, the world and God, and to to give salvation to the soul.

The way the religion manifests is temporary, depending upon the circumstances and consciousness of the people. When a manifested religion no longer serves its purpose, or becomes deteriorated or cor-

PERCEPTIONS OF REALITY

rupted, the supreme Lord sends his prophet to either evolve the existing religion or change it completely. In this way the consciousness of mankind is brought to another level. For example, when the Jewish rabbis became corrupt, God sent Jesus to evolve the existing religion. When the Vedic brahmans in India became corrupt, God sent Buddha to create a new religion.

The true prophet is a seer. In Sanskrit he is called a *rishi* (one who sees). The *rishis*, or true prophets, were the transparent medium for the eternal truths to descend into the material cosmos. By dint of the *rishi's* spiritual progress, they were revealed the inner worlds of spirit by the supreme Lord himself. The true *rishi* would open his heart and enter into the abstract mind, empty himself of the false ego and material conceptions and fill himself with the essence of spirit. This is revelation.

These revelations are divine and allow the *rishi*, or prophet, to see a level or aspect of the absolute truth. Not all revelations are the same. Depending upon the purity of the prophet and the circumstances of the time, the supreme Lord gives a vision of a certain aspect or level of the absolute truth. As we will see later, there are many different aspects and levels of the absolute truth.

The revelations of the prophets were transmitted in light and sound vibrations. The great seers perceived the inner meaning of the sound and light and therefore received a clear meaning of its purport. The vibrations that were received by the seers were not stagnant, but living and full of divine power. They were creative and formative. The divine seed syllables and light images which the prophets perceived grew within their purified minds and manifested as divine wisdom. The divine light and sound were transferred from the world of spirit into the soul of the seer, which then rose from his soul and empowered his purified mind to articulate the revelation into matter via the medium of sound vibration, or language. In this supra human com-

PERCEPTIONS OF REALITY

munication between the prophet and the supreme absolute truth, divine knowledge has been descending since time immemorial.

This form of descension of divine knowledge through revelation is not perfect. The first problem may arise when the prophet receives the revelation. If the prophet is pure in heart, free from false ego and material conditioning, then there will not be any distortion in the perception. But if the prophet is not pure in heart and mind, distortion may occur.

The next problem arises when the prophet tries to articulate the absolute truth into physical language. Physical language is a limited faculty which cannot fully grasp the unlimited potential of the absolute. Therefore the first distortions occur almost immediately.

The prophet will try to explain the teachings to his or her disciples. Depending upon the abilities of the prophet to teach and of the disciples to understand the spiritual concepts, the truth may again become distorted. Each disciple will grasp different meanings from the same teachings and give their own purports according to their own understandings, propensities, conditioning and personal agendas.

As we can see, the original absolute truth can begin distorting as soon as it comes into contact with material nature. Even so, considering the circumstances, this is the most efficient way to transfer the spiritual truths into our world which is dominated by ignorance. If the prophet is pure in heart, there won't be any distortion. If the disciples are also pure in heart, then again the distortions won't enter or will be minimal. But if there is impurity present, the results could be very noticeable.

The prophet will proclaim a new religious understanding amongst the masses of people from his divine revelations, which if are minimal in distortion, and if understood properly by the disciples and the people, will uplift their consciousness. The new religion will prosper for some time in its original form, but eventually it will undergo changes.

PERCEPTIONS OF REALITY

These changes occur either due to the ability of the people to follow the practices, adaptation to social and cultural customs, influences from other religions, misunderstandings of the original doctrine, additions and subtractions to the original doctrine, mistakes in the original doctrine, or even for political and personal agendas. Because of these changes, the original teachings change, forming diverse denominations and philosophies. Over an extended length of time, the original doctrines can change dramatically.

Even most of the ancient scriptures have gone through these modifications. There have been many interpolations, additions, subtractions, mistranslations, and even fabrications. These occur either due to lack of knowledge, misunderstandings, adaptations to social and cultural customs, the need to simplify, erroneous conclusions of the revelations (either by an impure prophet or the disciples) and even due to corrupted priests and kings for personal and political agendas. It takes a discerning eye to be able to distinguish the truth from the distortions in these scriptures. If one is situated in one's heart, then one can see if the teaching is coming from the heart or from some other source.

There are other problems in understanding the various holy scriptures, such as the changes of word usage through the ages. Another problem is that many times, passages are written in metaphors that are difficult to understand properly. Also, we must always keep in mind that the sages were perceiving these truths from a perspective of realization that is beyond our understandings. Because of these factors, the translators, commentators and readers can come to erroneous conclusions about their true meanings.

As we can see, it is very important for us, as individuals, to raise our consciousness to a higher platform, or perspective, of realization, so that we can discern the truth from the non truth, even in the various holy scriptures. One can raise his consciousness by following the principles throughout this book, which will direct one into the heart. From that position of consciousness, the abstract mind opens, which allows a different thinking process. In this state of consciousness, one can find the solutions to these problems.

In a "normal" state of consciousness, the world seems like a maze, so easy to become confused. We seem to be moping around in the dark, trying to find our way. When one raises his consciousness to a higher perspective, then that higher consciousness is like a light that shines in the darkness, so that one can find the correct path of truth.

In the great epic, the *Mahabharata,* the personification of religiosity quizzed King Yudhisthira, "What is the real path to follow in this life?" King Yudhisthira replied, "The real path in life cannot be ascertained by logic or argument, nor by reading the different holy scriptures. It cannot even be understood by consulting the various learned sages, as even their conclusions are differing. The best path to follow is in the cave of one's own heart, for this is the seat of true knowledge regarding religion."

The Basic Premises

To research reality, we must first of all have some initial premises which we believe to be true. These premises are the foundation upon which we can build our knowledge and understanding. These basic premises are that which we can all agree to be true.

The first premise is that each of us exists. We are all individual forms of consciousness that temporarily inhabit physical bodies. We possess a mind, an intellect, senses, emotions, feelings, hopes and desires.

Secondly, there is a supreme Godhead or universal energy from which we and this physical world emanate from. This supreme being or energy is also in supreme control of this material manifestation.

PERCEPTIONS OF REALITY

Then there is the material manifestation in which we find ourselves in. This world, and everything in it, is relative and subject to duality. Our bodies and everything else in the world exist for a temporary time. Everything in creation is subject to time. We are born, we grow, we procreate, we deteriorate and we die. As our bodies and mind change throughout life, there is one constant. That is our identity as a conscious being. Everything else in this material creation changes by the influence of the time factor.

The next premise is that we are conscious beings inhabiting physical bodies and placed in this material cosmos for a purpose. That purpose is to learn and evolve as conscious entities. These then are our basic premises that we will use as a foundation on which to build our knowledge upon.

Depending upon our previous conditioning, we will each have a unique foundation of knowledge, which creates the perspective in which to perceive ourselves and the world around us. Our conditioned perspective limits our perception. We must therefore evolve our perspective in order to perceive reality in a higher light. This next chapter will show how our perceptions are dependent upon our perspective, and how our perceptions can change by shifting our perspective to different levels.

PERCEPTIONS OF REALITY

PERCEPTIONS OF REALITY

2. Changing Perspectives

Our Binary System of Opposites

There are two fundamental opposing forces in nature. In the Toa they are referred to as yin/yang. One polarity is male; the other is female. The male energy is active and propelling. The female energy is receptive and impelling. This law can be seen in our physical law of magnetics: A magnet both attracts and repels, depending on its polarity.

If we could create a symbol for these polar opposites, it would be the number 10. It is a whole number comprised of two opposite halves: 1 and 0. The number 1 is linear; the number 0 is spherical. Two opposites together as one. The number one is linear, active and male. The number 0 is spherical, receptive and female. The linear, male energy is protruding outwardly into its environment. The spherical, female energy is an absorbing, impelling energy, attracting the male energy inward. This is evident in sexual intercourse. The male protruding energy is linear, and the male penis is in the shape of the number 1. The female energy is receptive and spherical, and the female vagina is in the shape of the number 0.

This symbol 10 also represents our binary system of mathematics, which is used in computer language. Two opposites comprise the entire system; 1 and 0. It seems simple, but there is no limit to this system except in the hardware and software. In fact, the entire material creation uses this same system to create reality. If we analyze further this symbolic code, it will open a doorway in which to view creation from a higher perspective.

Polarities and Perspective

A basic principle of polarities is that our perception of them shifts depending upon our perspective. We can experience that when it is daytime in Hawaii, it is simultaneously nighttime in England. Only our location (perspective) dictates the polarity which we experience (perceive). When it is summer in the Northern Hemisphere, it is winter in the Southern Hemisphere. If you stand on one side of the Hemisphere, the earth is spinning clockwise. If you stand on the other side of the Hemisphere, the earth is spinning counterclockwise; yet the earth is moving in the same direction. As you can see, it is our perspective which dictates our perception of polarity.

Let's look again at the symbol 10. What differentiates a linear line from a spherical line? It's only our perspective, but in another sense from our previous examples. In actual fact, there are no straight lines in nature. To prove this, let's look at the longest lines we can find; the grid lines on a map. We see straight lines going off into the four directions. But as these "straight" lines move outwardly in opposite directions, they bend, until they eventually meet at opposite ends of the earth. No straight lines here, only circles that eventually end at their point of origin.

As these "straight" lines bend around their orbits, their directions

PERCEPTIONS OF REALITY

may also change. If you started from the North Pole and flew directly south, north would be behind you. When you reach the South Pole you would then be moving north, with the North Pole ahead of you. This is all happening while you are traveling a "straight" line. You eventually end up at your origin. This can also be experienced in space, as we see all heavenly bodies orbiting in their respective paths.

Our thinking process can also be divided into linear thought and spherical thought. Linear thought could be compared to believing the earth was flat; spherical thinking could be compared to believing that the earth was round. If one believed that the earth was flat, he could justify straight lines in his reality. But if one was to fly off like an eagle and view his environment from above, he would see an overview of the entire picture. Eventually as one flies higher, he sees that all straight lines bend. Only by moving outside of our immediate environment can we see the whole picture.

As we overview our life/creation, we would see many separate incidences (straight lines) merge together to form the sphere of our total life/creation. From our present perspective we view our life and our environment as if they were moving in straight lines. They seem to be moving in a straight line, from past, to present, to future. Our life seems to be moving in a straight line, as do most things. In reality all this energy is spiraling; but we, as minute living beings, experience only a microscopic portion of creation. In this small sector of time and space the lines seem to be straight, hence we have a tendency to view ourselves and our environment as linear, especially in our male (linear) dominated society. In a sense, most of us are living our lives in a two-dimensional flat earth. We are not seeing the whole picture.

We can summarize this by saying that linear thought is like viewing a single portion of an object in detail. It is like a zoom lens or microscope. Spherical thought, on the other hand, is viewing the entire picture. It is a birds-eye view.

PERCEPTIONS OF REALITY
Perspective, Conception and Movement

Depending on our perspective, our conception of the world changes. In the spiritual world, God is in the center and the individual souls are the peripheral. When the individual soul turns his attention away from the supreme Lord and directs it towards the material nature, he takes on the false ego and sees a reflection of the real spiritual nature. In this reflection the principles of perception change. God is no longer perceived as the center, but rather each individual sees himself as the center. This creates confusion and chaos in the material world, because if each person perceives himself as the center, then we have many conflicting centers that are relative to each other. Each person then perceives the same material time and space in a different manner, in relation to his own conception of self as center.

This can also be experienced in the movements of the solar system. If we consider our planet earth to be the center of the cosmos as a stationary planet, then we perceive the sun, moon, planets and stars as orbiting us. This is called geocentric vision, which is relatively true. But if we were to view the movements of the solar system from outside the solar system, we would see quite a different phenomena. Our solar system is heliocentric. Nothing in time and space is stationary, including our planet earth.

Everything passes through time and space, including our planet earth. If the earth was stationary, then it would not pass through time, and it would then be in a state of dormant fixation. All heavenly bodies rotate in their respective orbits. From outside our solar system our planet earth can be observed as rotating on its axis daily, and as orbiting our sun on a yearly basis. Beyond this perception, from the perspective of the higher dimensional systems, the sun is again observed as orbiting the earth. So geocentric and heliocentric movements are relative to perspective and perception.

Perspective and Time

Where is here and now? The speed of light is considered the fastest movement of energy in physical space. If one could move faster than the speed of light, he would move outside of the present moment and enter into the future. According to Einstein's law of relativity, it is not possible to travel faster than the speed of light. We know that the speed of light is not instantaneous, so there is a lag of the present moment depending on one's location. For example, the light from the moon appears on earth approximately two seconds after it originates on the moon. The light from the sun takes about nine minutes to reach us, and the light from the stars could take hundreds and even thousands of years to reach us. So when is the present moment? It depends where you are.

A well known American physicist, Ruddy Rucker, explains this phenomena, "As far as we know, nothing travels faster than light. It is interesting to realize that you are never actually seeing the world *right now*. What you see is always slightly in the past, as it takes time for the light to get to you; what you hear is even further in the past; and smells travel even slower than sounds. You see the rocket's flash, you hear its explosion, then you smell the smoke. Your sensations, at any given instant, are all signals from various events from the past. Even what you feel and taste is not happening exactly now, as it takes some time for the nerve impulses to travel from your skin to your brain. To talk about 'all of space - taken right now' is really to speak very abstractly."

PERCEPTIONS OF REALITY

The Blind Men and the Elephant

There is an old parable from ancient India that shows how our perspective limits our perception. Once there were four blind men that came upon an elephant. The first blind man went to investigate and felt a tusk of the elephant. He concluded that an elephant is smooth, narrow and long, and that he was pointed at the end like a spear. The second blind man felt the trunk of the elephant. He concluded that the elephant was like a giant python. The third blind man felt the leg of the elephant. His conclusion was that the elephant was like a large tree trunk with hair. The fourth blind man felt the elephant's tail. He concluded that the elephant was like a thin hairy snake with a brush on the end.

Now each of these blind men concluded that the elephant was a different and even contradictory object, yet each of them were partially correct in their assumptions. This is because each of them perceived only a partial aspect of the entire object.

This parable gives us an idea of how limited our perceptions can be in describing our reality. In our assumptions of the material world, we are possessing a very limited perception of the complete reality. Each person perceives himself as the center of his universe, so his perceptions of reality are limited to his own personal perspective, which may be very different from someone else's.

Even if we looked at the perceptions of the entire human race, they are limited to our present scientific knowledge of reality. We are also confined to our tiny earth planet. There are billions of stars and galaxies that we know very little about. Our perception of the physical dimension of existence is very small. Beyond this physical earth dimension, there are many other finer, more subtle dimensions that very few people are aware of; and science doesn't even acknowledge their existence. As you can see, our limits of the material reality are very

PERCEPTIONS OF REALITY

small indeed. There are principles outside of our perception that are very different from our known world. Many of these are even contradictory. Our very limited knowledge of the world is due to the fact that we are perceiving only a partial view of a tiny sector of time and space of the entire cosmos.

This same analogy can be applied to our perceptions of the absolute realm. The majority of the prophets and sages perceive only a partial view of the complete absolute. They may be able to perceive one level or one aspect of the absolute, and they therefore conclude that the absolute has certain qualities. Now if we study the perceptions of the great sages and prophets, we can find many differences and many contradictory qualities of the absolute. This has given rise to many sectarian and philosophical arguments, what to speak of the creations of the separate religious doctrines.

Some sages describe that the supreme absolute is a great golden light. There are those who say that it is an all-pervading energy. Some describe an all-pervading intelligence, while others perceive him in the hearts of all living entities. Some report that the supreme is a father figure, while others report that the supreme is a mother figure. Some have revealed that the supreme absolute truth is a beautiful, ever youthful blue boy that plays a flute, while others state that the absolute is a vast emptiness. All of these sages are correct in there assumptions, as they have all perceived the absolute truth; yet they have described so many different and even contradictory conclusions. This is because they have viewed only certain aspects or levels of the same supreme absolute Godhead. They have each viewed only a partial manifestation of the complete whole. In the following chapter we will explore this in more detail.

As we can see, our limits of perception are tiny indeed. We are viewing a microscopic portion of the complete reality. In this tiny speck of reality, we perceive certain qualities and principles, and we conclude that we have a grand knowledge of truth. In reality, we know only very little about the whole of creation and even less of the absolute realm. There are many qualities and principles that are very different from what we can perceive.

Prelude to Perceptions

In the following chapters I will be giving insight into the three profound questions of humanity: "Who am I?" "From where have I come?" and "What is this place?" I will also be explaining a fourth question that humanity has become confused about: "What is the path?" I will be deciphering these questions from a higher state of consciousness - from revelation. I will explain these revelations in a way that is easily comprehended for those of us who are still perceiving the reality from the perspective of "normal" consciousness. In other words, I will be decoding the mysteries, so that we can grasp the concepts and thereby create a new foundation of understanding.

I will be presenting the perceptions of the great seers who were pure in heart, as well as my own perceptions of reality. These perceptions come from the self-evident faith, or revelation. In the past thirty years of my life I have practiced the life of meditation, contemplation, prayer, devotion, observation, experience, and the study of the previous *rishis*. When I look back on my life, I see how the Lord allowed me to experience a variety of events and circumstances to be able to reveal this knowledge to the best of my abilities.

Over the years many revelations were revealed to me. As I have described, revelations are not static, but are living and full of divine power. They are creative and formative. They manifest in the heart and then grow within one's consciousness. I then contemplated these revelations, wrote them down, worked with them, let them grow and compared them to the revelations of the past seers, prophets and

PERCEPTIONS OF REALITY

commentators who were pure in heart. These truths were then confirmed to me in different ways in my life. These are my perceptions of truth, which also correspond with the truth of the previous pure *rishis*. I hope that this will point you in the right direction so that you may perceive truth and God in your own heart.

Later in this book, I will be revealing in more detail the principles one may adapt in order to free one's self from the past conditioning that binds the consciousness to one's present perceptions. As you use these principles in your life, you will be able to make quantum leaps in consciousness. You will be able to shift your perspective to new heights of awareness, from which you will be able to perceive not only the answers to these three profound questions, but also the solutions to the rest of life.

PERCEPTIONS OF REALITY

OM Mani Padme Hum

Translation from Tibetan Sanskrit mantra,

"O Lord, O jewel in the lotus of the heart"

PERCEPTIONS OF REALITY

3. Perceptions of God

To begin this chapter I must explain that God is not a subject that is comprehensible to the intellect or mind. He is not subject to the laws of material nature, such as time and space, and he is beyond any logical conclusions. To try to define God would be to limit that which is limitless. As you will see, he has many inconceivable potencies that are not possible for mundane objects. Probably for this reason, many religions have left this topic blank. I will try to explain what I know from my own revelations, but mostly from the revelations of the previous sages. Keep in mind that you can never know God simply by reading about him, but only by experiencing him in your own heart. He is only visible by the faculty of the soul.

So Many Gods

Every religion has its own expression of who or what God is. He is called by many names: Jehovah, Allah, Krishna, Shiva, Nirvana, the Tao, The Great Spirit and so many others. Some people see God everywhere, or see him in everything. Some people see God in the heart

PERCEPTIONS OF REALITY

of all living beings. Some people see God as an impersonal energy behind everything. Many people see God as a person; some see him as a male, and others as a female. The Buddhists see God as Nirvana, and the Vedantists see God as the impersonal Brahman. Christians see God as a holy trinity, while Vaishnavas see God as the divine couple. So which of these gods is the true God? All of the above are correct.

There is only one God, one without a second, and all of the above are him. To understand the absolute truth, we must open our hearts and allow him entrance. When he enters, we can understand that the supreme Godhead is like a magnificent transcendental jewel with millions of facets. This magnificent multifaceted transcendental jewel reflects the one Godhead on each of its innumerable facets. Each facet reflects a different aspect of the one Godhead.

There is only one God, but due to his infinite potency, he manifests himself into countless forms. All of these forms are spiritual and transcendental. They are comprised of concentrated spiritual energy and are not affected by time and space. They are devoid of any material inebriates, and each of them is omnipotent (all-powerful), omniscient (all-knowing), omnipresent (all-pervading), full of all beauty and bliss, and is eternal.

The innumerable forms of Godhead are non different from himself. There are more forms of the supreme Lord than there are waves in the ocean, yet each of them is the same one and only God. This is all due to his inconceivable potency. He is simultaneously one and many eternally.

PERCEPTIONS OF REALITY

God is Simultaneously Personal and Impersonal

Many people engage in the controversy of attributing either definite form or formlessness to the supreme absolute reality. The proponents of divine form say that if the supreme Lord has no form, there would be no possibility of worship. Those who advocate formlessness to the absolute reality say that if the Lord had a form it would restrict his all pervasion. In reality both groups are lacking in proper understanding. The supreme ultimate reality is both with form and formlessness. Both mutually controversial attributes are present within the supreme Lord, due to his inconceivable potency.

For some people it may be difficult to accept that the supreme absolute can be a person, as this appears to be limiting, but look around at the wonderful variegatetness of this one planet. How can such a creation come into existence, with all of its order and beauty, without the faculty of sentience and intelligence? Sentience and intelligence denote personality. Also, if God was not sentient, then how can we, the minute living entities, have sentience? Sentience is an attribute, and if it is not found in the supreme absolute, then from where has it manifest? The forms of the Lord are not limiting, because they are composed of spiritual energy, which is beyond the confines of time and space.

The supreme Lord possesses both natures of form and formlessness. Those who believe in only one of these aspects and discards the other is said to be viewing with a single eye. The controversial discussions of form and formlessness are useless. The supreme Lord does not have a temporary material form, but an eternal transcendental form. The supreme eternal reality is beyond the controversies of the sects. The essence seekers need not become entangled in this controversy.

The Threefold Manifestation of Divine Potency

The supreme Godhead manifests into three primary potencies. The first of these potencies is sentience, consciousness, or knowing. In Sanskrit this is known as the *chit* potency. This is the expanding knowledge function. This potency manifests as the supreme consciousness in the innumerable forms of Godhead. This *chit* potency also transforms into the sentience of the innumerable individual spirit souls.

The second potency is the potency of bliss and love. This is also known as the pleasure-giving potency. In Sanskrit this potency is called *ananda*. This potency is manifest as devotion and the various transcendental activities, or pastimes, in the spiritual domain. In the material cosmos this potency is transformed into the various propensities of the conditioned souls and the activities of material nature. This is the female, or mother, aspect of Godhead.

The third potency is the potency of eternity and infinity. This potency is called *sat* in Sanskrit. This potency creates the manifestation of the spiritual worlds and the infinite accommodating space for manifestation. It also manifests the spiritual bodies of the supreme Lord, The spiritual bodies of the individual spirit souls, the impersonal Brahman effulgence and eternal time. This potency is transformed into material accommodating space, the material worlds, the material bodies of the individual souls and material time.

The supreme Godhead is the possessor of these threefold potencies and yet is never separate from these energies. There is never any difference between the possessor of these potencies and the potencies.

They are eternally united as one being.

His Inconceivable Potency

The supreme Godhead is the original absolute entity, and he is the origin and creator of everything else in existence. He creates all of the worlds, both material and spiritual, all of the individual souls, time, and the interaction between time, the souls and all of the elements.

The material cosmos is a transformation of the energy of Godhead, yet the supreme Godhead is not affected by this transformation. He remains whole, complete, unchanged and all powerful. An example of this is an alchemical touchstone, which by its energy, turns iron into gold and yet remains the same. Likewise, the supreme Lord transforms his innumerable energies yet remains unchanged.

The absolute Godhead is one. His natural characteristic is that he possesses inconceivable potency. His eternal and inconceivable potencies are manifest in four stages: His personal form, his impersonal effulgence, the individual souls, and his material creations. This can be compared to the sun, which also exists in four features. There is the personality of the sun God, the glowing sphere of the sun, the sun's rays, and the reflection of the sun's rays in other objects. The same way that the sun appears in its fourfold manifestation, the supreme Lord likewise appears in his fourfold feature. There is one eternal supreme Godhead, whose form is eternal, yet is possessed of different potencies.

There seems to be a contradiction in this matter between the Lord being one eternal absolute truth and simultaneously possessing inconceivable potency. For the supreme Lord however, nothing is impossible as a result of the fact that he has inconceivable power. Therefore the Lord's oneness with and distinction from his energy is said to be inconceivable.

PERCEPTIONS OF REALITY

In the Vedic scriptures of ancient India, there are many descriptions of the Lord's inconceivable potency. Below are two of them:

"The supreme Lord has neither an inside nor an outside, neither a front nor a back; yet simultaneously he is both inside and outside of his creation. In fact, he is the world itself."
(Bhagavat Purana)

"By me, in my impersonal form, this entire material cosmos is pervaded. All beings are rooted in me, but I am not rooted in them. And yet everything that is created does not rest in me. Behold my mystic power. Although I am the maintainer of all living entities and I am everywhere, still my very self is the source of creation."
(Bhagavad-gita)

Due to the inconceivable potency of the Lord, he is simultaneously distinct and non distinct from his creations. Everything is created by Godhead. He is the original fountainhead of all energies, and everything in creation, both spiritual and material, is part of God. There is nothing that exists outside of God. God is everywhere, and everything is a part of him, yet simultaneously there is a distinction. Although there is simultaneous oneness and distinction between God and his energies, there is never any separation. Separation only exists as an illusion.

All Opposites are Reconciled in the Absolute

This brings us to another potency of the absolute Godhead. In the material cosmos mutually controversial qualities are not possible for phenomenal objects, but the supreme reality is non-phenomenal. Therefore the perfect assimilation of innumerable mutually controversial qualities is not uncommon for the supreme Lord. In one sense, the supreme Godhead is separate from the material cosmos by the influence of the time factor, and yet simultaneously there is never any separation. When the Lord is accepted as the creator, it suggests the mutation of the immutable. If it is said that God destroys, inauspiciousness is observed in the all auspicious Lord. By saying that God exists, then the supreme Lord, who is beyond time and space, is observed within the range of time. Such matters are beyond the scope of human logic. This is one of the many attributes of the supreme absolute truth. One can accept the perfect assimilation of all of the mutually controversial qualities in Godhead by means of the self-evident faith of the soul, or revelation.

God is All-powerful

Another of the innumerable attributes of the supreme Godhead is the fact that he has infinite potency. Each of the innumerable forms of Godhead are equally powerful. There is nothing which is more powerful and nothing that is outside of the power of Godhead.

A certain philosopher called Zarahustra accepted the existence of two supreme entities, one holy and one evil, by advocating duality in his book Zendavesta. Zarahustra was a very old philosopher who preached In ancient Persia. His philosophy became so contagious that in the religion of the Jews and amongst the followers of the Koran it created an entity called Satan as a rival to God. This philosophy is erroneous, as there can never be an entity or anything outside of the control of the supreme Lord. The Lord has no rivals. Such philosophies are created from the imagination. What people call Satan is only the illusional individual's own propensity towards evil.

This evil nature is a misconception of consciousness. Certain people have given this propensity a personality and a name, and have given it power. In this way the concept of Satan actually exists within the minds of such individuals, created by their own imagination. This is all due to misidentification of the real cause of evil propensities. The real cause is in the individual, but due to not wanting to own this propensity, the individual projects the cause to something external.

Other Attributes of Godhead

The supreme Godhead is also omniscient, or all-knowing, Although there are countless universes, both material and spiritual, and even more countless individual souls, the supreme Lord knows all of these manifestations fully. This is beyond the comprehension of human thought.

Our known universe is composed of some hundred billion galaxies. Our galaxy, the Milky Way, contains about 400 billion stars. One of them is our sun, and orbiting that sun is our tiny planet earth, with billions of humans, and countless animals, plants, etc. The supreme Lord knows every thought and every action of every being in all of the material and spiritual universes, past, present and future. Such an ability is beyond the scope of any imagination.

The supreme Lord is omnipresent, or all-pervading. He pervades everywhere by the fact that all of his energies are non different from himself, including the material energy. He also pervades everywhere through his impersonal Brahman effulgence. This Brahman pervades everywhere without limit. It is an infinite aspect of Godhead. The supreme Lord also manifests himself as the supersoul, which is situated in the heart of all living entities. He again manifests himself in his personal form within every atom. In this way the supreme Godhead pervades everywhere.

The supreme Lord is composed of, and contains, unlimited bliss and love. This bliss and love is the propensity of Godhead. He is the proprietor of unlimited bliss and love, and he is full of and never in wanting of all bliss and love.

Unparalleled beauty is another attribute of Godhead. All of the transcendental forms of the Lord are composed of condensed spiritual substance which is far beyond the concept of our mind's capacity. The spiritual energy is self-luminous and is more beautiful than anything imaginable. The forms of the Lord can only be perceived by the soul, when it is free of the material conditioning. The supreme absolute is the all-attractive one, and we, the individual souls, are the attracted.

Our Limited Conceptions of Godhead

As we can see, God is infinitely great, and we are infinitely small. We are only atomic part and parcel of the absolute Godhead, so we can never know God in his complete wholeness. Even when we are liberated from the illusion, we can never know God in his entirety.

The supreme Godhead has innumerable, eternal, transcendental forms, but we, as embodied souls, cannot conceive of these forms. The faculties of perception of an embodied soul are dependent on the mind, the senses and the intellect. All of these are products of the material substance, which is limited. Whatever we can conceive is limited to the mind's capabilities. Our mind may be able to expand, but only to certain limits, and Godhead is unlimited. For example, we cannot actually conceive of eternity. We can somehow, with limitation, understand the concept, but we cannot experience it. Likewise with infinity. We can somewhat understand the concept, but we cannot grasp the actual experience.

PERCEPTIONS OF REALITY

The spiritual substance cannot be perceived with the material faculties of the mind, senses or intellect. The spiritual substance can only be perceived by the faculty of the soul, which is also of spiritual substance. So as long as we identify with the mind, body and senses, we are limited to their capabilities. When we become free from the binding and limiting qualities of material substance, and identify with the soul, then we can experience the spiritual energies of the absolute.

Whatever the mind can conceive in imagination is bound by material inebriates. So when we conceive of God with our mind, we can only conceive of a material imagination of God. The forms of the Lord are an absolute reality. But when we conceive of these forms in our minds, the eternal absolute reality becomes clothed in the limited material substance of imagination. It becomes a subjective concept that we can understand. In this way the absolute truth is perceived by our mind.

Did you ever notice that the Greek gods are dressed as Greeks; the Egyptian gods are dressed as Egyptians; the Hindu gods are dressed as Hindus; and the Mayan gods are dressed as Mayans? In fact, if you look at all of the gods of the various civilizations, you'll notice that they are all dressed according to the civilization that worshipped them. Each God and pantheon of each religion reflects the culture and consciousness of each civilization.

Our visions and revelations of gods and saints are also affected by our religious and cultural conditioning. A Catholic will perceive the absolute truth in a vision of Mother Mary or Jesus Christ. A Hindu will perceive a vision of Krishna or Shiva. A Buddhist will see Buddha. You don't hear of a Christian having visions of Krishna, or a Buddhist having a vision of Mother Mary. Our revelations and perceptions of the absolute become colored by our conditioning, preconceptions and belief structures. Does this mean that the aforementioned personalities of Mary, Christ, Krishna, Shiva and Buddha don't really exist? They do exist in eternal spiritual forms, but due to our preconceptions, they appear as we think they are. In reality, their eternal spiritual forms are inconceivable to the human mind.

The forms of the absolute are composed of spiritual substance and cannot be perceived by the material senses or mind. They can only be perceived by the soul. If one is pure in heart and mind, then the soul will be able to perceive the true eternal spiritual forms of Godhead. But even then, it would be impossible to describe those forms to a conditioned living being. It would be like trying to describe color to someone who has been blind since birth. It would be incomprehensible. As long as we are in this blinded state of illusion, our perceptions of the absolute truth will be clouded.

Other misconceptions of God are that he is an angry God, or a jealous God; that he demands that we act in a certain way, or he will punish or condemn us for wrong doings. There is no such thing as hell. There is no such thing as the devil. There is no such thing as judgment. God does not require us to do anything for him, as he is full of all bliss and knowing. He does not lack anything, as there is nothing that can exist outside of God. God is love, and as a loving God, he loves all of his children unconditionally. All of these misconceptions of God are created from the imagination. They are all illusions and have nothing to do with the ultimate reality.

The Demigods

Some ancient peoples and some modern cultures still worship pantheons, or many other mythological gods and goddesses, mythological beings, and nature spirits. Each God of a pantheon, mythical being or nature spirit represents either partial aspects of God, or are demigods. Demigods are individual souls that have been empowered by the supreme Godhead to help manage the material cosmos. The supreme Lord directs and controls the powers of the demigods. They can never act out of the jurisdiction of the supreme Godhead. They do not compete with each other, or create difficulties for each other. All of these mythological stories of the gods are either metaphorical or are created by the imagination.

Each demigod represents a certain power of the supreme Lord. For example: Apollo was the demigod of music, poetry and purity. Athena was the goddess of wisdom. Aphrodite was the goddess of love. Hermes was the messenger of the gods. The nature spirits represent the powers of God manifested in nature. There are many cultures who worshiped the sun and the moon. Many times, the personalities of the ancient gods and goddesses were descriptions of specific powers in metaphor. These demigods and goddesses, nature spirits and other mythological beings are perceived in different ways, according to the various civilizations and cultures.

Now we can understand that these manifestations are not the supreme Godhead. Some of them are partial manifestations, which are personifications of the partial powers of Godhead. Some of them are individual souls, who represent certain powers of Godhead manifested in the material realm. All of these demigods are material positions of power. Some gods are simply famous kings and heroes, who were very powerful, and were later deified. Others were just personifications of different aspects of the human psyche. All of these sub gods and goddesses have subtle material bodies, not eternal transcendental forms like the supreme Lord. Like everything else in the material world, they are also subject to time. They are not all-powerful or all-knowing, but are limited to their specific duties.

PERCEPTIONS OF REALITY

4. Who am I?

The Seer and the Seen

The form or object is perceived and the eye is the perceiver. The eye is perceived and the mind is the perceiver. The mind, with its modifications, is perceived and the self is verily the perceiver. But the self is not perceived by any other.

The objects of perception appear as various because of such distinctions as color, size, shape, length etc. The eye, on the other hand, sees them, yet remains one and the same. The different objects appear distinct from one another. The one characteristic of objects is their changeability. The characteristic of the seer is unchangeability. The objects change, but their perceiver (the eye) is constant.

Although the eye is the perceiver in relationship to the various objects, it becomes the object of perception in relationship to the mind. The eye is subject to changes in relationship to the mind. These changes include blindness, blurriness, sharpness and dullness. The mind cognates these changes, because it is a unity. The eye, on account of its changeable nature, is an object, and its perceiver is the mind.

The mind undergoes changes in state, such as desire, determination, doubt, belief, understanding, confusion, fear, anger, happiness etc. It is our consciousness of self which perceives these changes in the mind. Because of its changeable nature, the mind is the object of perception and consciousness is the perceiver. Consciousness perceives all these states because it is a unity.

This consciousness is the eternal witness of all internal and external changes. It is never born, neither does it ever die. It does not increase or decay. It is constant, and being self-luminous, it illumines everything else.

As we can see, it is only consciousness of identity that is constant. The body is constantly changing from birth to childhood, adult, old age and death. The mind is ever changing constantly. It is only consciousness which is constant and never changing. The consciousness is self-luminous, or spiritual. Consciousness is a quality of the soul, and being constant, it continuous after death. This consciousness is the witness, or perceiver, of everything else. It is the only constant principle in material nature.

There are a few definitive meanings of consciousness. One is sentience, or identity of self. The quality or state of being aware of something within one's self. It is this aspect of consciousness which is constant and never changing. The other definitive meaning of consciousness is a state of being aware of external things. Another meaning is the normal state of conscious life. Both of these aspects of consciousness are dependent on the mind, which is changeable. When we speak of evolution of consciousness, it is these aspects of consciousness that evolve.

Characteristics of the Soul

The spirit soul is part and parcel of the supreme Godhead, and is therefore comprised of the same substance, which is sentience. While the supreme Godhead is infinitely great, the individual soul is atomic in proportion. Both the supreme Lord and the individual souls are similar in respect of the quality of consciousness or animation, but dissimilar and eternally distinct in respect of the quantitative aspect. The Lord is the whole, and the souls are the parts. The Lord is infinite, and the souls are infinitesimal. God is the eternal Lord, and the souls are the eternal servants by their essential nature. The supreme Lord is the eternal attractor, and the souls are the attracted. The Lord is the supreme ruler and the souls are the ruled. In this way, there is similarity in the fact that the spirit souls are comprised of the same substance as the Lord, but there are eternal distinctions, due to the soul being an infinitesimal part.

Because the spirit souls are parts of God, they are comprised of the same substance. The form of the spirit soul is the *chit* potency (sentience, consciousness, knowing). If the form of the spirit soul is *chit*, or sentience, the propensity of the soul is *ananda* (bliss and love). In the natural unconditioned state, this propensity is directed towards Godhead. In the material conditioned state, this propensity becomes perverted and is directed towards the bliss of sense gratification. The spirit soul is also *sat* (eternal). There is neither birth nor death for the soul. It is a constant principle.

The Sojourn of the Soul

We, as spirit souls, have always existed. We were never born, as we originally existed beyond time and space. Originally we existed as an idea within the supreme Godhead, without manifested individuality, but in union. Our consciousness expanded homogeneously throughout the white light, or what is called the impersonal Brahman, or *Brahmajyoti*.

PERCEPTIONS OF REALITY

In the impersonal Brahman, there is no duality of subject and object, but only the subject, which is consciousness. Because there is no object, there is no perception, because for perception to exist, there must be a subject and an object. Without an object, there is nothing to perceive. Therefore in the state of Brahman, we do not perceive anything.

At a certain juncture (not influenced by time), the spirit soul becomes aware of his individuality. At that point, there is an awareness of "I am," or "I exist." At this point, the awareness, which was expanded throughout the impersonal Brahman without a central point of awareness, contracts into a central point of awareness. The ego, or sense of individuality, comes into existence. At this point, the soul perceives himself as separate from the Brahman.

The ego is non-expansive, but rather personal and localized, and therefore cannot exist in the expansive, impersonal Brahman. At this point, the soul, becoming aware of perceiving, falls out of Brahman and into material awareness. When this happens, the soul enters into the realm of time and space. This "new" ego then exists for sometime in a subtle material dimension of awareness known as heaven. In this space, the soul is nurtured by motherly souls, just as a newborn baby.

The soul has a magnetic quality, which when it comes into the material atmosphere, magnetizes material substance to it. When the soul is inhabiting the heavenly spheres, it attracts subtle energies. These include the false ego (misidentification of self), the intellect and the mind.

There is a difference between the true ego and the false ego. The true ego identifies himself as a soul, independent of and not affected by material substance. The false ego is when the ego identifies with a material body, either subtle (mind and intellect) or gross (the physical body). In the heavenly spheres, the soul identifies with the subtle

PERCEPTIONS OF REALITY

body of false ego, mind and intellect.

After being nurtured for some time in the heavenly spheres, the soul begins his incarnations in physical reality, where he accepts and identifies with the gross physical body. When he is placed within the womb of his mother, he magnetizes the gross elements of space, air, fire, water and earth. This becomes his temporary material body.

When the soul enters this world, there comes with it a definite sense of separateness. The soul experiences himself as the center of his existence and perceives everyone and everything as separate from himself. He then perceives everything in relationship to "I and mine." This illusional concept is experienced for the purpose of evolution.

The soul will then continue to reincarnate, in body after body, to learn lessons, evolve and grow. He will face many obstacles on his path, which he must learn to overcome.

When we speak of the soul evolving and growing, it is not actually the soul that evolves and grows, as the soul is a constant principle; it neither increases nor decreases. What we mean by the soul evolving and growing, is that the soul becomes more aware of what he eternally is. He awakens to his eternal nature and his eternal function of knowledge and love that is unbounded by the effects of the material energy. This next chapter will explain this principle in detail.

PERCEPTIONS OF REALITY

PERCEPTIONS OF REALITY

5. Eternal and Causal Nature

The eternal nature of a thing is its eternal religion. Nature springs up from the constituent or making of a thing. When a thing comes into existence, a concomitant nature goes hand and hand with the formation of the it. That nature is its eternal characteristic. When that thing becomes contaminated due to unforeseen events, or if it is perverted by coming into contact with another thing, then its nature is also changed or perverted. This changed or perverted nature, as it becomes nursed by the faculty of time, accompanies the thing and bears a resemblance to its original eternal nature. This changed or perverted nature is not inborn in it, but is causal or accidental. For example, water is a thing, and liquidity is its nature. When it turns to ice, solidity or rigidity becomes its causal property. Causation is not eternal, but temporary, and vanishes with the disappearance of its cause. But the original nature that springs up with the formation of the thing is eternal and remains latent when it is perverted or changed. In due course of time, due to favorable circumstances, the true nature of a thing assumes its normal character.

PERCEPTIONS OF REALITY

The derivative meaning of a thing is that which exists and conveys meaning. There are two types of things, spiritual and material. The spirit soul is a spiritual thing manifest by the supreme Godhead. It is a part and parcel of the Godhead and it is of the same substance, but in atomic proportion. That substance is known as the *chit* potency, or the cognitive faculty of awareness.

The eternal nature of this thing (the soul) is also identical to the supreme Godhead, from which it was manifest. That eternal nature or religion is love. This is known as the *ananda* potency. In its eternal state, it is devoid of any hindrance. It is pure and unadulterated. This is the natural state of the soul, and in such a position, the object of the love is singular. That love is directed towards the supreme Lord, from which he emanates. When the soul directs his love towards the supreme Lord, then the soul also automatically loves all other living entities, as they are all parts and parcels of Godhead.

Because the spirit soul is manifest from the marginal potency, it is atomic in size and liable to be covered by the material energy. When this happens, the soul becomes illusional, and its nature then becomes causal or perverted. The material energy is the cause of this perversion.

When the spirit soul becomes covered by the material energy, the original nature, which was singular love, becomes perverted into many various propensities. In this condition, the phenomenal mind predominates over the soul. When this happens, the self-illuminated knowledge of the soul becomes dormant, and sensual experiences of the material world are thought to be the real knowledge. There is a big difference between the self-illumined knowledge of the soul and the knowledge of sensual experiences. The transcendental knowledge is absolute and not bound by time and space. It is therefore eternal and all-pervading. The perverted knowledge is only a variation of the real knowledge.

PERCEPTIONS OF REALITY

When the material objects come into proximity of the sense organs, the image of the object will be absorbed by the senses. The mind and intelligence receive and keep these images collected. This is known as the retentive memory of the mind. These stored images provide the substance for imagination. Depending upon the acquired feelings, the mind builds its kingdoms of knowledge, its perceptions, its judgments, and decides good and bad etc. This activity is called rationalism. All of these activities are known to be sensory activities. When the soul becomes covered by the material energy, his knowledge undergoes this type of perversion.

The love-natured inclination, or propensity, of the soul also undergoes perversion and takes on a causal nature. Love towards the supreme Godhead is the eternal and natural inclination of the soul. This natural relation of the soul and God can be compared to the magnetic attraction of iron, the liquifying tendency of heat, the burning power of fire, etc. When the soul comes into contact with the material substance, the natural propensity of the soul, love of Godhead, becomes perverted. The singular natural propensity of the soul then becomes manifold depending upon the inclinations. A good analogy of this is like light passing through a prism. The natural propensity of the soul is singular and unity. It can be compared to the white light. The material substance can be compared to the prism. When the white light enters, or passes through, the prism, the white light is refracted into seven divisions of color: red, orange, yellow, green, blue, violet and indigo. These colors correspond to the seven chakra centers within the physical body.

In this way, our single natural propensity of love of Godhead becomes perverted into seven areas or divisions of propensity in relation to the seven chakras. These include the desire for security, the emotions and sensations, power and movement, compassion and mercy, expression, imagination and intelligence.

PERCEPTIONS OF REALITY

Our love then takes on different forms according to the object of the love. Love for wealth is called greed. Love for the opposite sex is called lust. When love is manifested towards the distressed, it is called kindness. Attachment towards loved ones is called affection. When it is applied towards a benefactor, it is called gratitude. When this love is uncongenially tempered, it is called enmity.

Due to the contact with the material energy, the eternal nature or inclination of the soul gets transformed into various forms, due to the various inclinations. These perverted forms are all the causal nature.

The original eternal nature, which is singular love, remains dormant in the causal state of the soul. It is never lost, but only dormant. When the soul becomes free from the association or influence of the causation (material nature), it then manifests its eternal nature again.

The true purpose of religion is to free the soul from the causal effects of material nature. As long as the soul identifies with the material coverings, his eternal nature remains perverted. As one involves himself in the practices of true religion, he will gradually free himself of the causal principle and awaken his dormant eternal nature, which is love of God.

6. What is this world?

The Framework of the Cosmos

We, as spirit souls, find ourselves embodied and existing in a physical universe. What is this universe? The Buddhists believe that this material cosmos is simply an illusion, but in actual fact, it is not an illusion; it is real. The illusion is our false perception of it. We perceive ourselves as a false ego and identify with a physical body which creates our false concepts of "I and mine" and our false conceptions of the world.

Everything is part of the supreme whole, including this material universe. There is nothing that can exist that is not part of the supreme whole. The supreme Godhead has three primary energies: spiritual, material and marginal. The spiritual energy comprises the forms of the Lord, the spiritual realms, his pastimes, and the Brahman effulgence. The material energy consists of the innumerable material universes. The marginal energy consists of the innumerable spirit souls. They are called marginal because they are a potency that resides between the spiritual and material energy. Although the spirit souls are spiritual in nature, because they are infinitesimal, they can become overpowered by the material nature. For this reason, they are called marginal.

PERCEPTIONS OF REALITY

The supreme Godhead has manifested the spirit souls and the material nature as different principles than himself, whereas the spirit souls and material energy are not different from him. This is a great mystery. In his personal form the supreme Lord is eternally different from the spirit souls and material energy, but he has entered into them in the form of his potency. Simultaneously the spirit souls and the material energy are never separate from God and are comprised of his energy. This simultaneous one and difference is evident between the Lord and all of his energies.

The material cosmos, as is everything in it, is temporary. It is created and exists for some time (a very long time: 311 trillion, 40 billion earth years, by the calculations of the great sages of ancient India). Afterwards it is wound up and another creation takes place. This is happening eternally.

Within the material cosmos are innumerable universes with many different dimensions of consciousness and many types of planets inhabited by living souls. In our universe, the lower dimensions of consciousness are the physical worlds, and above them are many dimensions of more subtle energies.

According to the Vedic wisdom, the material energies are divided into eight levels, or dimensions, of existence. The first and most subtle is called the Maha-tattva, which consists of all of the principles, or elements, of creation. This Maha-tattva is divided into two states of existence: Pradhana and Prakriti. The Pradhana is the subtle, undifferentiated sum total of material creation. When the time factor is injected, as the conglomerating principle, manifestation takes place and is called Prakriti.

When the time is manifested, material activities are caused by the Maha-tattva being agitated. When the Maha-tattva becomes agitated, the various elements manifest in sequential order. These include intelligence, mind, ether (space), air, fire water and earth. These elements correspond to the seven chakras in the human body and to the divisions, or dimensions, of consciousness.

When the Maha-tattva is being agitated by the time element, the false ego springs forth. This false ego is what illusions us to identify with the material body. The false ego transforms into the modes of creation and preservation. Later the mode of transformation develops. From this manifestation, matter, its knowledge and its activities come into play.

As the Maha-tattva manifests into creation, each level of manifestation includes the elements of the previous level. For example: When time is manifest, it is then present in all of the younger levels. In this way, each new level adds a new dimension to the existing levels. The supreme Lord adjusts all of these different energies from within, as the supersoul, and from without, as the time factor.

By the conglomerating principle, the Lord enters into the Maha-tattva as the time factor. Due to the influence of time, all of the separated living souls awaken and conglomerate into different material universes. The supreme Lord manifests himself into the center of each of the innumerable material universes. The shell of each separate universe is made of all of the material elements and is likened to a golden egg. This shell is invisible to our physical eyes, as it resides in a subtle dimension. Within this shell, the material elements and dimensions begin forming, first around the inner layer of the shell, with each subsequent element forming directly below it.

The first level of elements created in this shell is the Pradhana, then Prakriti; both aspects of the Maha-tattva. Time produces the next layer of false ego. The false ego becomes threefold with the active power of creation, preservation and transformation. This threefold false ego is the source of all of the younger elements, both gross and subtle. Depending upon the influence of the three modes of creation, preservation and transformation, the false ego is characterized as ac-

PERCEPTIONS OF REALITY

tive, serene or dull.

By the transformation of the false ego in the mode of creation, intelligence is born. The functions of the intelligence are to analyze in proper perspective, the power of discrimination, and the power to help the mind and senses to make choices. Other characteristics of intelligence are doubt, misapprehension, correct apprehension, memory and deep sleep.

From the false ego in the mode of preservation the mind is born, whose thoughts and reflections give rise to desire. The symptoms of the mind are to accept and reject.

The agitation of the false ego in the mode of transformation produces the subtle element of sound. From sound came the ethereal sky, or space, and the sense of hearing.

After the individual living souls received bodies of false ego, they received bodies of intelligence and mind. The bodies in these mental dimensions are thought formations. Each entity in those dimensions are unique thoughts. When sound was developed, space came into being with the sense of hearing. The individual souls could then take bodies, not only of thought, but also of sound.

In due course of time, the subtle element of touch was produced out of the ether. From this subtle element of touch came the element of air and the sense of touch. As Prakriti manifests, the subtle elements become more gross, or dense, and therefore different senses are developed to associate with the new elements. From the evolution of air, touch was developed in order to distinguish between hard and soft, hot and cold, pleasure and pain. The actions of air are the movements of the winds, the carrier of sound, and other sense perceptions. It also provides for proper nutrition of the body. By the interactions of air and touch, one receives different forms according to destiny.

When the air and the sense of touch are developed, the individual souls take on bodies of wind, later developing into form. From the evolution of form, fire is generated. From this, the sense of sight is developed, which sees different forms in color. The mind imagines the forms and colors, and with the interaction of sound, space, air and touch, different forms are produced according to destiny.

The characteristics of form are understood by dimension, quality and individuality. The form of fire is appreciated by its effulgence. The qualities of fire are light and heat.

The eyes, as the sense of sight, born of fire, see form and light. They also receive light, which is then transformed into photo currents (electrical energy) in the optic nerves. These photo currents then feed the hypothalamus, which regulates the bodily functions.

By the interaction of fire and the visual sensations, the subtle element of taste evolved. From taste, water is produced, and the tongue, or sense of taste, was then produced. We can perceive this on our tongue: The subtle element of taste makes our mouth salivate (water).

Taste then becomes manifest as sweet, bitter, astringent, pungent, sour and salty, depending on the contact of particular substances. The characteristics of water are as follows: The ability to moisten other substances, coagulating different mixtures, causing satisfaction, maintaining life, softening things, drive away heat, incessantly supply itself to reservoirs of water and to refreshen thirst.

By the interaction of water and the taste perception, the subtle element of odor is produced. From this emanates the element of earth and the olfactory sense. Hence we can smell the odors of the earth. Odor manifests itself as mixed, offensive, fragrant, mild, strong, acidic, etc.

The characteristics of earth are manifold. Each of the levels of elements also creates a separate dimension of consciousness. The element of earth creates the physical dimension that we, as human beings, live in. The physical dimension expands as far as the physical senses can extend. This means that all of the planets and stars visible in space are all situated in the physical earth dimension. Since the cause exists in the effect as well, the characteristics of the causes are also observed in the effects. Because of this, all of the elements, gross and subtle, exist on the earth plane. The physical dimension of earth is then a multi-elemental and multi-sensual projection of the finer elements/ dimensions of creation. When all of the material elements become manifest, the material creation becomes complete.

The Seven Hermetic Principles of Creation

According to ancient history, Thoth Trismegistos appeared in history three times. He appeared first as Thoth, the Atlantean priest (later deified in Egypt), then as Hermes, and then as Archangel Michael. All three of these incarnations gave humanity the science of geomancy (our interrelationship between heaven and earth). In the *Emerald Tablets* of Thoth, the seven universal Hermetic principles are summarized as follows:

The principle of mentalism: The creation is simply a projection of the infinite supreme Lord. This material manifestation is produced by the thought of the supreme Lord. The famous philosophical work, the *Vedanta-sutra* states, "Brahman is the direct cause, because the texts show that the material elements were produced by his reflection, or thought." In the *Bhagavad-gita,* Lord Krishna states, "The seven great sages, and before them the other great sages, were born out of my mind, and all sentient creatures in these planets descended from them."

The principle of correspondence: Whatever is above, is like that which is below. This is also stated in the *Bhagavat Purana*, "As a grain of wheat is divided into two parts, and one can estimate the size of the upper part by knowing the size of the lower part, the expert geomancers instruct, one can understand the upper portion of the universe by knowing those of the lower part."

The principle of rhythm: Everything moves in cycles. As energy moves through space and time, it moves through cycles. Some cycles are experienced as day and night, weeks, months, seasons, years, etc. As the spirit souls move through time, they also undergo the cycle of repeated birth and death.

The principle of vibration: All energy is composed of different frequencies, which vibrate. Everything in creation vibrates at its own unique frequency.

The principle of polarity: Everything is dual in nature; everything has pairs of opposites. This principle of duality is experienced in all phases of creation.

The principle of causation: Everything has a cause and an effect. This is known as karma. Everything and everybody is under the control of karma in this material cosmos. "As you sow, so shall you reap."

The principle of gender: Everything has both a feminine and masculine aspect.

These seven principles of creation are universal and exist in all dimensions of material consciousness.

Time

Eternal time is the primeval source of the interactions of the forces of nature. Time is unchangeable and limitless, yet everything changes as it passes through time. The material manifestation is separated from the supreme Lord by the means of time, yet simultaneously the material creation is never separated from the supreme Lord.

Metaphysically, time is distinguished as absolute and real. Absolute time is continuous and is unaffected by the speed or slowness of material things. Time is astronomically and mathematically calculated in relation to the speed, change and life of a particular object. Factually however, time has nothing to do with the relativity of things; rather, everything is shaped and calculated in terms of the facility offered by time. Time is the basic measurement of the activities of the senses, by which we calculate past, present and future. But in actual calculation, time has no beginning or end.

The experience, or perception, of time is relative to one's consciousness. We can experience this daily. Notice that when you're having fun, time seems to be flying by, and when you're bored, it seems to be dragging on forever. Only our perception of time dictates how we experience it.

Time can also be defined as a form of relationship between the embodied souls and the phenomenal nature. Extensive study of this subject by the advanced seers shows that time is actually non sentient. Time is often explained as an influence or instrument of the supreme Lord. It is considered an impersonal feature of the Lord. Investigation of the principle of time clearly indicates that time is an attribute due to the relation of the sentience with the material nature. It is manifested due to the relation of the embodied souls with the material nature. Therefore at the association of the sentience, the feeling of awareness of the existence of material nature is called time.

The Material Cosmos is a Perverted Reflection of the Spiritual Cosmos

The spiritual world is eternal, infinite and fully conscious. The material world, on the other hand, is temporary, finite and full of illusion. The material world is a reflection of the spiritual world, and as any reflection, there are similarities and differences.

If you look into a mirror, the reflection appears the same, but there are many dissimilarities. Not only is the reflection not the same, but there are many opposite properties. In the mirror your right side is reflected as your left side, and vice-versa. In the mirror your reflection is flat, or two dimensional. The reflection has no power of movement. It is dependent on your movement. Also the reflection is not conscious, whereas you are.

The spiritual world is fully conscious, whereas the material world is unconscious. It is only the presence of spirit that is conscious within matter. The material energy has no power of movement. It is only the presence of spirit that causes movement (the sentient principle is situated within every atom as an expansion of the supreme Lord). The spiritual world has unlimited dimensions, whereas the material world has limited dimensions (our physical reality is three dimensional). In the spiritual world there is no encumbrance of space. In our physical world only a certain amount of objects can fit in a defined space. If a table is situated in a space, you must move it to put something else in that space. In the spiritual world this is not a problem. Everything can fit into one space. In fact, although the spiritual world is infinite without restriction, the entire spiritual world is simultaneously situated within the center of every atom.

Now if the material world is a reflection of the spiritual world, the spiritual world must contain variegated objects. If the spiritual world consisted only of the white light of Brahman, then the reflection of that white light would not be able to reveal variegated objects.

Throughout the Upanishads and Puranas there are numerous descriptions of the spiritual realms. There are descriptions of cities, parks, rivers, lakes, sky, trees, plants, flowers, birds, animals and people. All of these spiritual objects are free from the influence of material time and space. The spiritual time is the eternal now, and the

PERCEPTIONS OF REALITY

spiritual space is unlimited and non confining. It is described that all of the spiritual objects are eternal, conscious, alive and full of all beauty, knowing and bliss. All of the spiritual objects are self-illuminating with brilliance, and everything scintillates like the eye of a peacock. Every word is a song, and every movement is a dance. There is never any want, anxiety, sickness, old age or death. This world lies beyond our senses, mind and intellect, and can only br perceived through the faculty of the soul.

Our Perceptions of the World

Some people perceive the world as a prison house, where the soul is bound and caused to suffer for his sins. Other people perceive the world as a playground in which to enjoy and play. Others perceive the world as a schoolhouse in which to learn lessons and grow. Depending upon your perception of the world, it becomes that for you. It depends only on your choice of perception. If you choose to see it as a prison, it becomes a prison.

I prefer to see the world as a schoolhouse, where I can learn lessons and evolve to a higher state of awareness. In this perception I see God as a loving parent and teacher, and I see the creation as a wonderful, beautiful manifestation of God's energy.

For those who view the world as a prison house, they may harbor bitterness and resentment. They will feel bound, without any sense of free will and control of their lives. They may also subconsciously perceive God as the warden and perceive the creation as a place of misery. They may harbor resentment and other negative emotions towards God's creation and want to escape. This state of existence binds the soul and restricts its evolution. The creation is God's creation, and therefore is a part of God. By harboring resentment towards God's creation, one is indirectly harboring resentment towards God

PERCEPTIONS OF REALITY

himself. This is also a pessimistic view that gives little joy.

For those who perceive the world as a playground, they will avoid the lessons and obstacles presented to them to further their evolution. They will usually choose pleasure over pain regardless of the situation and consequences. On the good side, at least those who choose this perception view God's creation in a positive light.

Therefore the world becomes either a prison house, a schoolhouse, or a playground, according to our perception of it. Our perception of the world also magnetizes certain energies and situations which will fortify our concept or belief of the world and ourselves. If we were to believe that the world was a prison house full of suffering, then we would draw to us circumstances which prove our belief system. Even if good things happen, we would perceive them as suffering just to justify our belief.

If we believe we are unfortunate, we will draw misfortune to us. On the other hand, if we believe we are fortunate, we will magnetize good fortune to us, and see good fortune in our experiences, even in experiences that others perceive as unfortunate. Our belief structures create our perspective, which then creates our perception. This magnetizes situations to support our beliefs by sending out frequencies of energy that resonate with similar energies that become attracted to us.

Our perception dictates whether we will be either happy or miserable. I have known persons with extreme wealth, who were miserable, always complaining, arguing and criticizing. I have known other people who owned very little, and yet they were very agreeable, never complaining or arguing; always appreciative and seeing the good in everything. These persons were always grateful for what little they had, and were always kind and gracious.

We can see two distinctly different attitudes, or states of mind. One is satisfied, the other is unsatisfied, and as we can see, neither of these attitudes were dependent on the present external circumstances. In

PERCEPTIONS OF REALITY

fact, the persons who had the most to be grateful for were the ones who were least grateful. The only difference between these two states of consciousness is perception. Do you perceive the glass as half full or half empty?

PERCEPTIONS OF REALITY

7. The Subconscious World

So far, we have concentrated on the conscious part of creation, but there is a hidden half as well, just as there is a hidden half of the moon. There is also a hidden part of each of us. Every night when the moon shines, we sleep and dream in the darkness of the night. Moon, darkness, night, sleep and dreaming all pertain to the subconscious part of our being and of creation herself.

We spend many hours in each daily cycle in sleep, but how many of us actually consider what happens to us while we are sleeping? Every night, when we sleep, our mind, intelligence and false ego all leave behind the gross body (made of earth, water, fire, air and space). In effect, we leave our body and enter the dream state. There are two types of sleep: deep sleep and dreaming. When we first fall asleep, and several times throughout the night, we enter deep sleep. In the *Brahma Upanishad* there is a description of deep sleep, "One in dreamless sleep enters into the state of one's abode, where the indwelling deity resides. This state of consciousness is a reflection of *samadhi*, just as the moon reflects the light of the sun." *Samadhi* is the goal of consciousness from practicing meditation.

After this deep sleep, we enter into the dream state. In this dream state, our mind, intelligence and false ego have accepted a new body -

PERCEPTIONS OF REALITY

a dream body. We experience this phenomena every night. When we awake in the morning, we find ourselves in our familiar physical body, ready to resume another day of conscious activities on the physical plane. We enter this cycle every night when we are tired. When we awake in the morning, we find ourselves refreshed and ready for another day.

Just as our conscious material world is a reflection of the spiritual world, this subconscious dream state is another reflection of our conscious state. It is associated with water, and just like when you look at your reflection in water, it has a fluid quality. The ripples in the water also cause distortion of the reflection. The subconscious state is likewise a distorted reflection of our waking state. Like water, our dream state is very fluid, and because of this fluidity, the dreamscape and activities can change dramatically. Just like on earth there is a foundation and in water there is no foundation; likewise, in our physical world there is foundation, and in the subconscious world there is no foundation. Because of this, our consciousness is lowered into a stupor-like dream state so we will not become too aware and alarmed. Even so, we can have some pretty harrowing nightmares.

As in any reflection, there are some reversals of properties and images in these subconscious spheres. Because the subconscious is a reflection of the conscious creation, the polarities are reversed. Just like when you look in a mirror, your right hand becomes your left and vice-versa

There are certain phenomena that occur in nature that, if studied, give us an idea of the structure of the subconscious world. Notice that if you stand on the earth, that the sun appears as a small orb of light above you that radiates outwardly and covers the earth. The earth is then surrounded by the sea. This creates a situation, when perceived on land, where the sun is in the center, the earth surrounds the sun, and the sea surrounds the land. If we look at the way our

PERCEPTIONS OF REALITY

heavenly bodies orbit, we see the same order: The sun is in the center, our earth orbits the sun, and the moon orbits the earth.

In our conscious day, the sun is in the center, as it is above us in the center of the land and again in the center of the solar system as we orbit it. In our subconscious night, the sun isn't even present. Our moon is present, which reflects the light of the sun, just as the subconscious self reflects the conscious self. At night the moon isn't in the center. Our earth is in the center and the moon orbits us (the earth). So what exactly does all of this mean? These two luminary bodies, the sun and the moon, represent the ego, or self. The sun represents the waking, conscious self, and the moon represents the dreamy subconscious self. The earth represents our body. In our waking consciousness, we experience our self/ego inside our body, viewing outwardly our sensory existence. The self/ego (sun) is in the center, and the body surrounds (orbits) the ego (sun).

In our subconscious world, we experience differently. In our dreams, the ego surrounds the dream body, just as the moon (subconscious ego) orbits the earth. Our dreams all take place within our individual ego, separate from other egos. Whatever we dream at night is all parts of ourselves. In Jungian psychology it is explained that all the persons in our dreams are aspects, or sub personalities, of ourselves. Whatever we dream at night is only an extension of our own individual ego. So our subconscious self (the moon) surrounds (orbits) the dream body (the earth).

This subconscious world is an important part of ourselves, as it gives us the opportunity to understand ourselves and our lessons in life. It offers us a perspective of our conscious life - a reflection. Just as the moon reflects the light of the sun (ego) to shine on areas of darkness, likewise our dreams reflect the light of our conscious self and offer us the chance to view portions of ourselves that are in darkness.

PERCEPTIONS OF REALITY

In the *Vedanta-sutras* and commentaries there are descriptions of the dream state, "The ideas of the waking state are not like those of the dream state, because they are of a different nature." "The objects of the dream state do not have the same characteristics of the waking state. The objects perceived in the dream state are memories of the waking state. In the waking state they are perceptions, not memories. The objects in the dream state can instantly change form, and are found to be unreal upon awakening. Although the objects in the dream come from memories, this is only a partial statement of fact. It is the supreme Lord that actually creates the objects in the dream state, and makes the soul experience them. They are therefore also real, only the difference is that the Lord creates them for a temporary purpose and for a particular soul only; while the external world he has created for all of the souls and has given them greater fixation."

As we can see then, the dreamscape is produced by the Lord for the individual. In Jungian Psychology it is explained that dreams are a way that God speaks to us in symbolic form. It is a form of primeval language of symbols. By learning to read the symbols, what they mean to us individually, we can listen to God as he instructs us in our sleep. By using the principles of Jungian psychology, such as dream therapy, we can deal with the subconscious conditioning that manifests in our lives as issues, patterns, phobias, depression etc.

There is another aspect of our subconscious self besides our dreams and deep sleep, and this is the dark side (meaning hidden) of ourselves. It is from this part of us that manifests our underlying patterns and deep seated emotions. Just like in a reflection, the polarity is switched. If you are a man, your subconscious self is a female, and vice-versa. This hidden part of our consciousness is always crying out to us for balance in our lives. It is our dreams that reveal to us this subconscious world.

There is a transference of energy between the waking conscious part of our existence, and the subconscious part of our being. The energies of the conscious self are reflected and merge into the subconscious, and it is then reflected, or manifested, back into our conscious self.

This subconscious world is an important part of our lives, as it gives us the opportunity to understand our lessons in life. It offers us another perspective of our conscious life - a reflection. Just as the moon reflects the light of the sun (ego) to shine on areas of darkness, likewise our dreams offer us the chance to view the portions of us that lie in darkness.

PERCEPTIONS OF REALITY

8. What is the Path?

The Soul's Itinerary

The spirit soul's existence in the impersonal Brahman is ever expansive, but as an atomic portion of Godhead, the bliss in the Brahman is also only atomic. This bliss is called *brahmananda*. At the point that the consciousness of the spirit soul becomes aware of itself as an individual, the soul leaves the Brahman effulgence and enters the material cosmos. In this state of existence, the spirit soul enters the region of time and space and experiences the duality of pleasure and pain. When the soul comes into contact with the material substance, the memory of *brahmananda* is lost and the soul identifies with the material mind and body. He then wanders throughout existence searching for bliss, which is the soul's inherent nature and propensity.

Due to the perception of illusion, the soul searches for bliss in the phenomenal mundane objects and tries to avoid pain. This is the evolutionary process that each soul must traverse to reach his goal of reunion with the supreme Lord. In the soul's subsequent incarnations, he is given different sets of lessons depending on the situation and advancement of consciousness.

The goal of this process is to regain our spiritual nature and reunite with the supreme Lord. This is the meaning of yoga (to unite). When the goal is achieved, the spirit soul is no longer limited to the atomic portion of bliss which is experienced in the impersonal Brahman effulgence. Instead, the spirit soul is endowed with a much greater propensity, or ability, to experience bliss. When the goal is achieved, the spirit soul retains his identity as an individual, yet he is simultaneously united to Godhead. This union expresses more bliss than can be calculated as compared to the bliss of the impersonal Brahman.

When this happens, the spirit soul is aware that his position of retaining his identity and simultaneously being united with his Lord was an eternal situation. This is because there are no time factors of past, present and future in the spiritual reality, but only the eternal present. This is a great mystery that many commentators have failed to understand. The spirit soul, when he is situated in his spiritual position, becomes conscious of that which eternally is. He sees his soul as a thread of light emanating from the impersonal Brahman, passing through the material cosmos of space and time, through many incarnations and into the spiritual domain, where his spiritual identity is in union with the supreme Godhead. Thus he has attained his goal of the evolutionary process, which is to awaken to one's eternal nature.

Free Will or Destiny?

Do we have free will, or are we bound by destiny? This is a question that philosophers have argued for millennia. If we don't have free will, then we are bound to a specific path that we have no power to change. We have no control over our lives, and we are forced to live a life that has been dictated to us. Our choices in life would be only an illusion of choice. Yet destiny reveals itself many times. Astrologers will argue that a person's life can be ascertained by his birth chart. They can show time lines that match a person's life. It is also said that the supreme Lord controls every action. Do we think that the person we marry is a coincidence? That our children are by chance? That the experiences in life are random events? How many circumstances in our lives seem planned by destiny? The threads of destiny seem to be woven within the tapestries of our lives.

So which is true? Do we have free will, or are we bound by destiny? They both are true. We have free will, yet simultaneously, we are bound by destiny. We can use the analogy of a bird in a cage. A bird is bound by his cage; he cannot escape. But within the cage, the bird can fly around, eat, sleep, etc. The cage is our destiny, and within that cage, we have the free will to act in different ways. But our analogy ends there.

In life our destiny was created by our free will. We do have the free will to choose. By our choices, we perform various actions. By our actions, we create karmas, or reactions. These karmas create our destiny. We become bound by these karmas. Our parents, our spouse, our children, our work, where we live, our religion, society etc. - all of these are manifested due to our karmas, which were originally created by our free will. All of these manifestations (parents, spouse, religion, society, etc.) help create our conditioning and beliefs. So by our karmas we also create our conditioning and our beliefs, which also help form our bondage to a certain destiny, as they force us to act in certain ways.

In other words, by our free will, we create karma, which creates circumstances, which are part of our destiny, which then create our conditioning, which also is creating our destiny. Now this destiny that we have created forms the path we must follow in life. By our karmas, the path may be smooth or rough, and our karmas also dictate

PERCEPTIONS OF REALITY

the direction the path leads to.

Our destiny forms a barrier, and we are forced to stay within its boundaries. But within those boundaries, we still have some free will. Although we do have this free will, by the influence of our past conditioning and beliefs (which help define our destiny), we are forced to act and think in certain ways in most of our activities. Generally, when we perform actions, they are usually conditioned responses. So in a sense, we are practically bound by destiny in so many ways. We do have some freedom in which we can make certain choices, but even these choices will be influenced by our conditioning and beliefs. So although we do have the free will to choose, most of our choices are influenced by our conditioning, and therefore are also bound within our destiny.

So how do we become free from this bondage? It was our free will that originally created our destiny, and by the use of our free will, we can also change our destiny. We have the free will to choose, and if we can make conscious choices that are not influenced by our conditioning, we can change our direction in life. We can choose to perform different actions. By our actions within the boundaries of our destiny, we can change that very destiny. We have within us the power and the free will to perform various activities that can change our lives, such as prayer, meditation, devotion, giving in charity, etc. These actions have the power to change our destiny.

We also have the power and free will to think differently; to change our perceptions of reality. When we change our perceptions of the world, we can change our conditioning. When we change our conditioning, we are actually changing our destiny. We will be able to change the direction of our path in life, and we can also make it smoother.

It all boils down to one thing: our ability to change our mind; to make the right choices. Although we are bound by our destiny, we can change it by changing our consciousness. Every moment is an opportunity to change our life around. It is a matter of making different choices. We do make choices all the time, but our conditioning always makes us choose the path of our destiny. If we can become conscious enough to not choose according to our conditioned responses, but rather from a higher perspective, then we can change our path. We see this happening all the time; people changing their lives around by making different choices and then acting on those new choices. We see drug addicts and alcoholics stop their substance abuse. We see people leave abusive relationships. These people are changing their destinies.

This is the path of higher consciousness. It is all a matter of being conscious and making conscious choices. By choosing things that are for our highest good, then we are breaking free of the bonds of destiny, and we are creating a new path to follow. We are no longer choosing according to our past conditioning. We are then creating a new destiny. When this happens, the external world reacts by magnetizing different energies towards us. The world is set up to accommodate these changes. It is within its parameters to be able to shift its matrix to adapt to these changes of patterns. Each of us has within himself the power to change his destiny. It is a matter of choice.

Educational System as Analogy

There is no one exclusive path in this evolutionary process. Each person is a unique individual and each is situated in a different level of evolution. What is right action for one person may not be right for someone else.

A good analogy would be to compare it to our modern education system, which includes preschool through postgraduate studies. Different types of lessons and knowledge are given to students according to their abilities. For example, although algebra may be a true knowledge, it would be a ridiculous waste of time to try to teach algebra to first grade students.

According to the learning abilities of the students, a certain level of knowledge is presented to them to learn. When they master one level, they can then proceed to the next level of learning. Another aspect of school is that there are different subject matters: history, math, science, etc. If a student is presently studying math, it would be irrelevant to include history topics at that time. When the math class is finished, then the student could begin his history lessons.

With this analogy we can understand how each person has different lessons according to his level of understanding. He is also given different types of lessons at different times. One person may be dealing with issues of anger, so certain lessons will be placed before him to deal with those issues. Another person may be dealing with self-esteem issues, so his lessons would be of a different type.

By understanding how each person is at a particular level of advancement, we can also become free of judgment. Just as we cannot harshly judge a first grader for not understanding algebra, likewise, we should not judge others just because they haven't reached an acceptable (by our standards) level of evolution in their lives.

Whatever path you find yourself on in life is perfectly orchestrated for your evolution. I will try to explain some of the pitfalls and detours that create difficulties on one's path. By avoiding these problems, one's path can become smoother. You can follow this advice or not. Some people find that they must experience the lessons to learn them, while others can learn by listening.

Understanding One's Nature

To choose one's path in life, one must understand his own nature.

Each person has a certain type of nature which produces certain propensities. One person may have a propensity to be a doctor, another an engineer, and another a farmer. It is imperative to understand one's nature as a human being and choose a vocation and lifestyle accordingly. Otherwise, a person will feel great dissatisfaction in life.

Many people choose a vocation against their nature simply for the purpose of the accumulation of money. This kind of choice in life will not bring ultimate happiness. Even the money earned from such endeavors will not bring any lasting happiness. We can experience this everywhere around us. We see so many people who are dissatisfied with their occupations. Many people even hate their jobs. Are you one of these people? Did you know that research has shown that disliking one's job is a major risk factor in the cause of heart attacks? Disliking one's job can also lead to alcohol and drug dependence, frustration, dispassion, anger and resentment.

So the first and most important thing one must do to progress in life is to learn and understand one's nature. Then one must choose an occupation and lifestyle that will fulfill the propensity of that nature. This may take some time. Aptitude tests, counseling and experience are good ways to learn about and understand one's nature.

Celibacy?

Another topic to investigate is one's inclination towards family life. Many spiritual paths demand celibacy from their followers, which may be the inclination for a very few people. But for the most part, we, in our present culture, are not suited for such a lifestyle. To take to the path of celibacy without being suited for such a path will never bring any good results. To try such an austere path for most people will only cause problems and eventually a fall from such a false posi-

PERCEPTIONS OF REALITY

tion. If one is not qualified for such a path, the following of that path would be a path of denial. This brings with it anger, bitterness, tenseness, false pride, prejudice, envy and dissatisfaction.

Many people choose a path of celibacy due to issues involving their sexuality, and some people are even repulsed by sex. We must understand that attraction and repulsion are two sides of the same coin. As long as one is repulsed by sex, then one is not free from it. It is far better to accept counseling and therapy concerning such issues, and create a life that is more balanced and beneficial for one's evolution. One must always be absolutely honest in his or her self evaluation. It is important to accept where one truly is, and gradually evolve from that platform, rather than to pretend to be something that one truly isn't.

Married life is actually a beneficial path for advancing our consciousness. There are many good lessons one can learn from marriage. For example, one must learn about sharing, considering other people, commitment and responsibility, tolerance, give and take, nurturing, love, kindness and so many others. Marriage gives us a wonderful opportunity to work on ourselves in so many areas of our lives.

Our spouse also becomes a mirror for us, to see what we need to work on in ourselves. So, if you are married and are having difficulties with your spouse, start looking inside yourself, and see what you need to change about yourself. Your spouse is only making your internal hang-ups apparent. In other words, it's not necessarily your spouse, it might be you. When you change, you will be surprised that your spouse will change as well, because he or she no longer needs to mirror that image.

False Austerity

Austerity and renunciation are the practices of retracting the sense organs from the sense objects. A certain amount of retraction can be good for one's spiritual advancement, but one must be very careful not to renounce any more than one is comfortable with. If one retracts the senses organs from the objects of the senses, and yet the mind still thinks of the pleasure of the sense objects, then that person is deluding himself and is only a pretender. False austerity means to renounce more than what is necessary. This is done either to try to force, or speed up, one's spiritual advancement, or for false prestige. Such false platforms cannot help one advance in consciousness.

The paths of true austerity and renunciation have been designed for certain individuals who have progressed in their evolution to a point of being able to let go without being adversely affected by the consequences. Because they have tasted a higher, spiritual taste, they can easily let go of the pleasure of the sense objects. This is postgraduate work. If one tries to follow the path of renunciation without the proper qualifications, it will cause anger, bitterness, frustration, envy, condemnation and guilt, and it will turn one's heart to stone. One will lose his compassion, mercy, and the ability to love. Without these finer qualities, one's spiritual evolution becomes hampered. The true path is the middle path of moderation. One should accept where he truly is at the present time, and gradually, step by step, progress from that point.

Sense Control

This doesn't mean that we shouldn't control our senses. On the contrary, sense control is part of the process of evolution. As one evolves in consciousness, the senses and mind eventually become controlled. When this occurs, the mind and senses become obedient servants to consciousness.

When the mind and senses are out of control, we, the consciousness, become slaves to them. Our mind and senses desire so many things, and they drag us hither and thither to satisfy them. The problem is that they can never become satiated. Therefore we run after one gratification to another trying to find happiness in momentary pleasures.

The secret in life is to find balance, and this also applies to sense gratification. We must find balance between work and play and in all aspects of our lives. The process of sense control must be a gradual process. If one was to renounce too much gratification too quickly, it would knock the mind and senses out of balance and cause undo stress.

This stress eventually causes the individual to fall from this level of false renunciation, causing the pendulum to swing in the opposite direction. This also causes guilt, which brings other problems. Anyone who has tried a crash diet has experienced this.

I have personally witnessed hundreds of spiritual aspirants take to an austere lifestyle, renouncing all forms of sense gratification. Eventually almost all of them fell from that position. The problem is that even though the senses are retracted from the sense objects, the mind continues to think of them. Such fruitless endeavors eventually, due to internal stress, cause anger, jealousy, frustration, guilt and eventual fall from that false position.

Nature is always striving for balance, because balance is preservation, and preservation is necessary for existence. When something is out of balance, the forces of nature always strive to bring it back into balance. It acts like a pendulum. To bring the energy back into balance, it swings back in the opposite direction. So if one was to engage in false austerities, the pendulum of nature will swing back to the other direction of excessive sense gratification until the energy is balanced out.

This also pertains to those whose senses are out of control. Eventually nature will create situations that will crash down on them and put them into a state of sense depravation. Such situations can be illness, prison, financial disaster, divorce, etc.

So the secret is to follow the advice of the Buddha and live a balanced life, and gradually, step by step, slowly bring the senses under control. This is easier for some than for others. We need to practice with small things at first, one at a time, always paying attention to the stress that it produces.

Desire

Desire springs forth from the center of our being. Not all desires are bad. On the contrary, it is desire that improves our lives and evolves our spirit. Without desire we would have little reason for existence. It is a function of our innermost being, and no one can be totally free from it.

Many desires spring forth from us constantly. The ego, with the help of the mind and intellect, choose which desires to dwell upon, which to act upon, and which to let pass out. Some desires are weak and can be easily pushed out by the rational mind, or they leave on their own, but other desires are strong and won't disappear. If we dwell upon a desire, it creates a dwelling in the mind for these desires to dwell. They then attract more desires of the same type to fortify the original desire. If we continue to dwell on these desires, eventually the internal mental pressure will cause us to act out the desires.

But there are many desires which are neither good for us nor for others. Such desires, if acted upon, would cause difficulties, pain, delusion and even devastation. These desires need to be dealt with. They are obstacles that need to be overcome. Bad habits, addictions, the desire to harm ourselves or others etc. are all obstacles we need to overcome, and lessons we need to learn.

If we try to fight a strong desire head on for a length of time, it will create an internal conflict which may create mental and emotional imbalance and disease. By fighting a desire, we are actually giving it energy. When we suppress a strong desire, it will still remain in the mind and spring forth again. The ways to deal with such powerful desires are by therapy, counseling, hypnosis, and spiritual activities like prayer, devotion and meditation.

The Only One Way Syndrome

Another topic to discuss concerning one's path is religions and spiritual leaders who proclaim that their path is the only true path, and that all other paths are false. Such conclusions are always based on misconceptions, misjudgments and/or personal agendas. Many times religious leaders will try to instill fear amongst the people by proclaiming that all those who don't follow their path will fall from grace and even go to hell.

In the past centuries some of the Christian missionaries and Moslem invasions were based upon this principle, and millions of innocent people have died for these beliefs. Such beliefs are not based on love, mercy and compassion, but rather ignorance, separatism, fear and the desire for power and wealth. These false conclusions are only distortions of the truth and are used to manipulate the masses into subjugation for the welfare of corrupt ruling and priestly castes. For the desire of power, wealth and subjugation, millions of people have been manipulated in this way with the use of fear and guilt. Whatever this has to do with the purpose of true religion, I cannot tell you.

For those that believe that there is only one way, then I have a question. Why does God allow his children to be born in a situation where that only one way is not available to them? Are these innocent people to be condemned or sent to a hell for something that they have no control over?

The Divisions of Spiritual Paths

In the famous philosophical treatise, The *Bhagavad-gita*, The supreme Lord Krishna describes the divisions of spiritual paths. These paths are called yoga, or that which unites. He explains to his disciple Arjuna that all of the forms of yoga he is describing ultimately lead to the same goal, which is union with the Lord.

He first describes the process of sankhya-yoga, or the metaphysical path of analytical study of the material nature. He then describes karma-yoga, or the yoga of action. This is the path of performing activities and utilizing the fruits of the activities for spiritual upliftment. He then describes jnana-yoga, or the path of divine knowledge. This includes the study of sacred scriptures and selfless action. Then he describes dhyana-yoga, or the path of meditation. At last he prescribes the path of devotion, or bhakti-yoga.

He tells Arjuna that of all of the yogas, this path of devotion is the easiest to perform and offers the quickest results. Another advantage of the path of devotion is that it is the eternal nature and function of the soul. In this way, devotion becomes both the means and the end. Because it is our eternal nature, our evolution must bring us to this point of awakening our dormant love for God and all of his children. So, although all of these spiritual paths can ultimately bring us back into union with God, once we have obtained that union we must cultivate devotion, because it is bhakti, or devotion, that is the only activity in the spiritual realm. The other paths are no longer necessary in the spiritual realms, as they were only bridges to help us get there, but devotion is both a bridge and the destination.

These different divisions of yoga are established to accommodate the various natures of different people. These divisions of yoga have many variations, as we see in the fact that there are so many different religions. But all forms of true religion will follow one or more of these divisions in their own specific ways. For example, both the Moslem and Christian religions offer the paths of devotion (bhakti-yoga), contemplation (meditation, or dhyana-yoga), the study of sacred scriptures and selfless action (jnana-yoga), and working for the church and giving in charity (karma-yoga).

Universal Actions and Qualities

Regardless of what division or path one accepts for his evolution of consciousness, there are many universal actions and qualities that we must each strive to develop. These qualities are found in all true spiritual teachings and can be used as a barometer for gauging our spiritual evolution. If you want to judge your own advancement, it is imperative to be completely honest in your evaluation. Many people are expert in being pretentious in their exhibition of these qualities, either from self deception or for the acquisition of honor and prestige.

Some of the actions that uplift our consciousness include prayer, meditation, contemplation, worship and devotion to God, giving in charity, helping those in need, guiding others, cleanliness, studying spiritual topics, chanting of mantras and devotional songs etc.

Some of the holy qualities we should strive to develop are compassion, mercy, kindness, nonviolence, gratitude, tolerance, modesty, honesty, courage, fortitude, forgiveness, equality, fearlessness, magnanimity, peacefulness, simplicity, respectfulness, friendliness to others, and freedom of self prestige.

Finding One's Own Path

Each person has a unique path in life. This path should not be dictated by others, such as family, friends, society or church. It is not necessary to conform to other's wishes about how one should live his life. As we can see, there are many paths to follow, many differing philosophies and religions, and many other options. So which path is the one for you?

As we have discussed, the first and most important thing one must ascertain is one's nature. Then one must decide if marriage is the correct choice, and then there is one's occupation to consider. One must also consider one's spiritual practices. How should one go about deciding these things?

Counseling and therapy can help, but to actually understand the correct path for each individual, there is truly only one direction one must follow. That is the direction into one's own heart. As King Yudhisthira said, "The real path in life cannot be ascertained by logic or argument, nor by reading the different holy scriptures. It cannot even be understood by consulting the various learned sages, as even their conclusions are differing. The best path to follow is in the cave of one's own heart, for this is the seat of true knowledge regarding religion."

To understand your true path, you must spend time in contemplation, and you must reach into the cavity of your heart. When you truly enter into your heart, you will automatically see your life and the world from a much higher perspective. By following the principles in the next chapter, you will be able break free of the conditioning that binds you to your present perception of life. When this happens, the

PERCEPTIONS OF REALITY

world will interface with you in a way that corresponds to your new and higher perspective of consciousness.

We will be seeing how to get in touch with our heart by simple, yet very profound, principles that anyone can follow. The beauty of these principles is the fact that once we clear the problems of our past conditioning, they're gone. We can immediately feel and experience the difference in our consciousness and our emotions. We can then use the same techniques in all of the situations in our lives. The more we clear our past conditioning, the more clear we will become, and the higher our perspective will reach.

PERCEPTIONS OF REALITY

9. The Great Secrets of Perception

In this chapter I will explain in more detail the science of how to change your perceptions of reality. These principles are simple, profound, and powerful. They can enable you to make a quantum leap in consciousness. I will show you how to release your past conditioning and belief structures. When this happens, your consciousness will be able to reach new levels of perspective that will enable you to perceive the world in a different manner. I will show you how to access the abstract mind and learn how to create a new life. When your consciousness changes, so does your external environment. You will begin to attract different energies into your life, and the external world will interface with you in a different manner that will bring you joy and harmony.

The secret is that you must use these principles in your life. They will not work simply by reading about them. You must first of all have the desire to change. You then have to spend the short amount of time necessary to do the exercises. If you only spend half an hour a day for one week doing these exercises, your life will change dramatically. Don't pass this opportunity by. The choice is yours.

PERCEPTIONS OF REALITY

The World is Perfect

There is a great secret to understanding this world and our placement in it. That secret is in our perception of it. By perceiving a certain truth about the material cosmos, we can become free from many of the difficulties we face in life. It is a simple truth, but one that is not easily comprehended, and one that is even more difficult to face. That truth is this: The material cosmos, and everything in it, is emanating from and is perfectly orchestrated by the supreme Godhead and is therefore ultimately perfect.

There is a famous verse from the *Isa Upanishad* that describes this quality, "The supreme Godhead is perfect and complete, and because he is perfect and complete, all emanations from him, such as this phenomenal world, are perfect and complete. Whatever is produced by the complete whole is also complete in itself. Because he is the complete whole, even though so many complete units emanate from him, he remains the complete balance."

There is nothing that exists outside of this perfection. This secret is very difficult to understand. We see around us war, hunger, disease, strife, confrontation, pain and destruction of all kinds. How can we see this as perfection? To grasp this concept, we must be able to look deeply into the situation to see past the seemingly imperfections that we experience. We must look at the purpose of creation, which is for the evolution of the soul. The soul evolves by overcoming obstacles and learning lessons, so a perfect world must include obstacles and lessons. We must understand that there isn't anything that happens to us that isn't perfectly orchestrated by the supreme Godhead for our growth and evolution.

We must also understand that we are occupying a miniscule sector of time and space. As individuals, we may occupy maybe a hundred years of time. We have history going back some thousands of years,

PERCEPTIONS OF REALITY

but we really don't know for sure how these previous people lived or felt. We don't know our past lives or the past lives of other people, and we don't know what is happening in the higher dimensions of consciousness. We don't know the bigger picture of life, so we really can't judge what is happening now. Because we don't have all of the facts concerning the circumstances that have led to the present now, our perception of reality is partial at best.

The material energy, by its innate nature, is always striving for balance, and balance is a quality of perfection. It is this balance that preserves nature herself. By contemplating nature, we see that she is always balancing herself. Her energy is never one-sided.

Whatever occurs in life is always balanced out. Because we exist in a microscopic portion of creation, we don't always see this in the big picture. Our miniscule sector of time and space is an infinitesimal portion of creation, and therefore we usually experience only one side of the scales at any given time.

But if we try to perceive the innate and perfect balance in nature, we will find it. In every failure there is a success. With every loss there is a new gain. With every disappointment there is a new opportunity. The opposite is not always apparent, as sometimes it takes time for the opposite balance to manifest.

For example, let's say your husband left you. At the time there was great remorse and anguish. But then sometime later you met someone else, got married and had a wonderful marriage. If your first husband didn't leave you, the second marriage would not exist. Also, other factors balanced out the energy as well. Perhaps it ended the fighting and arguments. It gave you time to reflect on what you did wrong in the marriage. You may have learned lessons about relationships. You may have become a better person for it. It gave you freedom, time for yourself, time for other things, etc. If we look at every failure in life and every disappointment, we can see how the energy

PERCEPTIONS OF REALITY

balanced itself, sometimes immediately, but sometimes it takes time to notice.

For every negative situation, there is always a positive outcome on the other side of the scales. It is not always easy to see this, especially while one is emotionally involved from a traumatic event. This may not be the time for trying to see the perfection. There is always time needed for grief, anguish, and reflection that one must experience in any traumatic situation. This is not the time to express to someone about the perfection of the universe. The perception of perfection may come later in time.

One thing to take into consideration when we try to see perfection is the subject of karma. Karma is not a form of punishment as much as it is a form of education or correction. It is a way that nature balances the scales. Whenever there is an action, it is the effect of a previous action, and it then forms a new reaction. These reactions are continually balancing out, and this balancing takes place over lifetimes. We, in this microscopic portion of creation, do not see this happening. Therefore we see bad things happen to good people, and because we can only perceive a small sector of time and space, we can't see the reasoning behind it.

The way that karma works on us is very subtle. When we perform an action, it sets us up for a reaction; good, bad or mixed. The action creates what is called a *vasana* in Sanskrit. A *vasana* is a subtle imprint on the mind. They appear in us since time immemorial. In other words, since the moment we enter the material time and space. These *vasanas*, or subtle imprints on the mind, give rise to thought. They attract specific external and internal energies towards us, and they move us into the direction necessary to receive the karmic reaction.

This is all part of the perfection of creation. The world is perfectly orchestrated for us to learn our lessons concerning our actions through the principle of *vasanas*. By changing, or uplifting, our con-

PERCEPTIONS OF REALITY

sciousness, we can actually change our karma by dissolving the *vasanas*. This is possible because the lesson has been learned. This potent action automatically balances the scales of karma.

Every time that there is a tragedy, there are always lessons to learn, and sometimes it is a repayment of karma. We should not judge these situations, because many times tragedy will befall a person and it has nothing to do with karma. It may be a situation the soul has voluntarily accepted to learn lessons to evolve.

Behind every cloud there is a silver lining. There are always benefits to every negative experience. When we perceive this perfection, a wonderful thing happens. We can understand the reasons for the occurrence of the situation and how we or others have benefitted. When this happens, the negative emotions, which were charged by our experiences, disappear. When the negative emotions disappear, something else manifests in its place, and that is gratitude. Gratitude is a powerful emotion that opens the doorway to new possibilities. It awakens one's latent potential. When we honestly feel gratitude, the heavens open up before us and shower us with gifts.

As long as we perceive failure, loss and sorrow in our lives, we become conditioned by these perceptions. These perceptions then bind us, not allowing us to move forward. We fail to see the perfection in the world, and instead become bitter, fearful, angry, resentful and doubtful. These negative emotions magnetize to us similar energies that will create similar circumstances which will then create the same emotions. In this way our perception of the world fortifies our belief structure. We believe the world is full of suffering, therefore that belief magnetizes more suffering to us to prove our belief to be true.

We must break free of this vicious cycle by perceiving perfection and balance everywhere. This cancels out the emotional charges related to the previous misfortunes, which then frees the energy. This stops the magnetic affect of attracting more misfortune and allows us to move out of the cycle. Our belief system then changes; we believe in perfection. Therefore we will perceive perfection, which then attracts positive situations which prove the perfection, which in turn will create the emotion of gratitude.

This doesn't mean that we shouldn't have compassion or show mercy and kindness to those who are suffering. Their suffering is real and needs comforting. We must always try to comfort those in need. If we don't express mercy and compassion, then our hearts become like stone, not allowing love to enter. We must find the balance and that is to feel compassion and kindness while still observing the perfection of the world.

The External World is a Reflection of our Internal World

By changing our perceptions, we can actually change our world. Our world and our life cannot ultimately change only by external actions, because the external world is simply a reflection of our internal world. Whatever is going on inside of us will manifest in the external world.

This is also a perfection of our world. Whatever is going on internally is reflected externally so we can perceive the problem. If we have internal conflict, it will manifest as external conflict. If we try only to stop the conflict in the external world, without addressing the internal conflict, then other external conflicts will manifest to continue mirroring the internal. If we have internal peace, it will manifest externally in our lives.

So if we want to change our world, then we must change what is going on inside ourselves. This is the most powerful concept given to

PERCEPTIONS OF REALITY

humanity to create a world of harmony, yet so many people try to avoid it. It seems easier to just blame someone or something else for our difficulties, but in reality it isn't easier but much more difficult. By pushing the blame outside of ourselves, we try to disown the responsibility. But in reality the responsibility always rests in our own selves.

As long as we push away the responsibility to outside of ourselves and blame external people and circumstances, then we will not be able to learn the lessons involved. The difficulties will remain in our lives. We may externally push one difficulty away, but it will return again in a slightly different form, because the real difficulty is situated inside ourselves. Until we understand the reality of the situation, accept the responsibility and work on ourselves internally, we will never be released from the difficulty. It will just keep manifesting externally, like a mirror, until we finally get it.

As soon as we begin to take responsibility for our own lives and our own problems and begin trying to correct them from the inside, a wonderful thing happens. We finally understand that we have control over our own lives. We become aware that we are not completely controlled by external circumstances, but rather we have a choice in our destiny. We can actually change our lives.

When we do this with even one situation, it opens a door. This door shows us the possibility of using this principle in every other situation in our lives. We can then move swiftly through our evolution of consciousness and we will feel a sense of true freedom. Consider this: When you push the blame and responsibility outside of yourself, it creates a bondage. As soon as you accept the responsibility and correct yourself on the inside, then you become free.

By accepting the responsibility and changing our inner being, all of the problems in life can be taken care of, and we can evolve into higher and more joyful states of consciousness. The choice is ours.

PERCEPTIONS OF REALITY

The World is as We Perceive It to Be

This brings us to the next great secret of perception: The world is as we perceive it to be. We discussed earlier how if we perceive the world as a prison house, or a school house, or a playground, it becomes that by magnetizing certain energies to support our belief system. This quality of perception goes even deeper. For example, if you perceive yourself as a failure, you will constantly set yourself up for failure. Whatever you are afraid of, that fear will attract that energy to you. If you harbor doubts, those doubts will manifest.

These thoughts, feelings and emotions are energetic, and they magnetize other energies with the same resonance. These thoughts, feelings and emotions have different degrees of strength, and the stronger they are, the more they can attract. Emotions have stronger charges than thoughts. When we combine the thoughts with emotions, this creates feelings, which create the strongest type of energy. The downside of this is that it is usually the negative thoughts, feelings and emotions that have the strongest charges. The emotions of fear, anger, hate and enmity are all powerful emotions that are usually combined with thoughts. Because of this, these negative emotions draw to us energies that resonate with the energies of the emotions and cause havoc in our lives.

We can try to be positive in our lives, always thinking of success and fortune, but then there are those nagging doubts and fears of failure, pessimism and poverty that keep poking their heads up and eventually ruin us. We need to balance these energies by working on ourselves, by rooting out the negative emotions that continually damage our lives. We need to perceive the perfect balance of energies in all of our experiences. Remember what we spoke about earlier: With

PERCEPTIONS OF REALITY

every failure there is a success, for every loss there is a gain, for every disappointment there is a new opportunity.

Look back on each of your perceived failures, losses, fears and disappointments and try to find the positive outcomes of each of them. What did you learn? What positive things came from them? Dig deep into yourself to find the positive benefits of each painful situation. By contemplating each of these past situations like this you can perceive the balance of the situation. It no longer is perceived as a failure, disappointment, or loss, because you now perceive something good that came from it. When this happens, it discharges the negative energies and emotions so they won't have the power to set you up in the future. By following this principle, you are actually changing your belief structure and conditioning. Your perception of the situation has changed. It is no longer a negative experience. When this happens, you become free from the bondage that your previous misperceptions created.

There is another secret to this formula. As I mentioned, thoughts combined with strong emotions have the most powerful charges. This is why deep prayer, done in the proper way, is so powerful. By praying with strong intent, a focused mind, strong feelings and emotion, the energy generated is incredibly powerful for changing our lives. If we pray with love in our hearts, then the power generated is unparalleled. By praying in this manner one can produce miracles. Even the powerful emotions of fear, anger and doubt can be destroyed by the power of such prayer. If one was to do this regularly, say two or three times a day or more, the changes could be miraculous.

Now that we are beginning to understand the physics and magnetism of energy, I am going to tell you something extraordinary: We, as a human species, are capable of much more than we believe. We are capable of performing miracles. It is our conditioning and belief structure that hold us back in this "normal" way of life. We perceive

PERCEPTIONS OF REALITY

the world in a certain way, and it becomes that. Our past conditioning creates our belief structure, which then creates the perspective from which we perceive reality. Our belief structure then magnetizes certain energies that resonate to our belief structure. Then our mind, intellect and senses interpret and translate the information of the energy to conform with our belief structure.

As a child we were taught that the world operates in a certain way, so we believed in it and it became thus. We were told our limitations, they were programed into our genetics, and our society and religions gave us limitations and taboos. We were forced to live lives in conformity with society and to be average. What if I were to tell you that it was all a misconception?

The world isn't as it seems. It is only a reality of energies, all of different frequencies, that our mind translates into a perceived reality, and that perception is based on and limited by our conditioning. We believe in struggle, so we struggle. We believe that conflict is a means to obtain what we want, so we engage in conflict. We believe that we don't deserve to be happy, so we're not happy. We believe that we must work hard and tow the party line to be successful, so we do. All of these are only misconceptions that we have created, and the world interfaces with our beliefs to create the world that we believe to be true.

We really don't need to struggle. The lilies of the field are not struggling. We don't need to resort to conflict to obtain what we need. There are other, nonviolent ways. We do deserve to be happy. God would like us to be happy, but we don't believe it. We could all be living joyful lives, if only we believed in it. If only we could change our beliefs, the world would change to accommodate them.

We believe we can't fly, so we can't. We believe we can't walk on water, so we can't. We believe we are going to grow old, so we do. There are yogis in India and many other places that can fly and walk

PERCEPTIONS OF REALITY

on water. Jesus walked on water. There are yogis that live for hundreds and even thousands of years in the Himalayas. There are even yogis that are immortal, such as Babaji. Jesus healed the sick and brought Lazarus back to life. There are many healers throughout the world that heal deadly diseases by touch and prayer.

Throughout the world there are shape shifters who can change their form or other forms at will. They can change their own form into a tree or a rock or a bird. These are not just stories but actual facts that have been documented by those who have visited the "less civilized" parts of the world. The shape shifters can change form, because they understand and believe in an underlying reality beyond the apparent reality that we believe in. They believe that this world is a dream time, or a projection of energy, much like a hologram, and they have the power to form portions of it into other shapes. In other words, they can perceive the higher dimensions of consciousness, and they can travel to those dimensions. From that perspective they can then restructure the elements to manifest specific portions of reality to form in the physical dimension.

Jesus said that if you had the faith of a mustard seed, you could move a mountain. What does he mean by that? A mustard seed is a very tiny seed, and a mountain is a very large object. What Jesus was saying is that it only takes a little bit of faith to do something very large.

So what is it that keeps us from being able to perform these miracles? It is our conditioning and belief structure that distort our perceptions. We may consciously try to believe that we can walk on water, but our subconscious conditioning doesn't believe it and sends us flags of fear and doubt. As long as we stay glued to our past conditioning and refuse to perceive the world from a higher perspective, then we will always be just average or less. We will be bound by the limitations that we have created and society has put on us. These limitations are like shackles that bind our consciousness to a life of little satisfaction and even less potential. There is a reason for society to bind us like this. It makes for better slaves to run the machine.

The mind is a very powerful tool. It has the power to shape our lives. Take for example the placebo effect. A doctor gives someone a sugar pill, and tells him it will cure his illness. Now we all know that sugar pills aren't going to cure anything, but the mind believes it to be a curative medicine, and the person becomes healed of the illness. This placebo effect has been documented over and over again. So what is it that cured the illness? It was the perception of the mind. The mind believed the sugar pill could cure and it did. Our belief in something has the power to make it so. Our doubts, on the other hand, have the power to not make it so.

It is now time for us as human beings to reach for our potential. It is time to perceive the world in a new light; to become what we are meant to be. I encourage you to step out of the normal consciousness; to step out of the shackles and perceive a new future for yourself and others. A future filled with joy and happiness. A future filled with prosperity and love; a future that your children and your children's children can inherit.

The Physics of Perception

Because we believe in certain facts about the world, then the world appears as such. But in reality, it is of a different nature. For example, according to physics, the physical reality is composed of about 99% total volume of space between the atoms. Yet when we place our hand against a tree, it feels very solid. It looks solid, as do our hands. So why is it solid, if in fact it's mostly just space? What gives objects in the physical dimension the quality of solidity is the electromagnetic fields that the objects produce. For example, a tree creates an electro-

PERCEPTIONS OF REALITY

magnetic field that creates the quality of solidity, therefore we cannot pass our hands through it.

The reality of the world is that it is made up of various states of energy that create frequencies of electromagnetic energy fields. According to the famous physicist David Bohm, this energy projects a certain reality, very much like the holodeck on the television show *Star Trek, The Next Generation*. It is just like a hologram, only it is multi-sensual. A hologram is produced by passing a laser through a holographic film, which then generates a three-dimensional image. Now an amazing property of holograms is that if you break the holographic film into many smaller pieces, and pass the laser through one of the smaller pieces, the image it produces is the original whole image. For example, if you had a hologram of an apple, and you broke the film into many pieces and passed the laser through a small piece, you would get an image of the whole apple.

Now if the physical reality is actually a multi-sensual holographic projection, then what this means is that each miniscule part of the universe contains all of the information of the entire universe. Each small body in the universe, from a planet, to a human, to a cell, to an atom, all contain this information. They are all microcosms of the macrocosm. This is explained in the *Emerald Tablets* of Thoth as the principle of correspondence: "As above, so below"

Now if each miniscule part of creation contains the information of all of the creation, then it must be imbedded in some type of code. It is that code that allows for the interaction of the various parts of creation with each other. Science is beginning to realize that each of the cells in our human bodies contains intelligence for interacting within the body, and that our mind is not limited to our brains, but it is also pervading in every cell.

I believe that this idea goes even further. I am suggesting that every particle of creation is conscious and contains an intelligence that in-

PERCEPTIONS OF REALITY

teracts, or communicates, with the supreme intelligence of the macrocosm. Every atom has encoded within it an intelligence that is hardwired to the supreme intelligence. This would explain the strange phenomenon of non locality. The fact that a subatomic particle on one side of the universe can instantaneously (faster than the speed of light) affect another subatomic particle on the other side of the universe. I believe that there is an all-pervading intelligence that interacts with every particle in creation. I believe this intelligence is God.

I believe that God is interacting with every atom to create a certain reality that conforms to our own individual belief structures. This is occurring in all of the dimensions in creation. Each successive higher dimension of consciousness is more subtle than the dimension below it. Our physical earth dimension is the most dense of the dimensions. By the interactions of the energies in the higher dimensions, the physical dimension takes its form. This physical dimension is then the multi-elemental, multi-sensual holographic projection of the finer energies of creation. So this physical dimension is the end result of the interactions of much finer energies, which are all being controlled by the supreme Lord. This is occurring due to the fact that the Lord is internally present as the supersoul within every body and every atom. He is also externally present as the time factor. By the interaction of these internal and external forces, creation takes its form.

But what form is it exactly? According to our own individual conditioning and belief structures, the reality interfaces with us to create a specific reality that conforms to our individual beliefs. Our thoughts, emotions and feelings then magnetize to us certain energies that resonate to our belief structure. Let's look at how this is happening.

The world, in reality, is composed of various states of energy that produce frequencies of electromagnetic energy fields. Our sense organs come into contact with these electromagnetic energies and transfer the information to our brain. The brain then transforms/ translates

PERCEPTIONS OF REALITY

the information into a reality that the mind and intellect can comprehend and is in accordance to its belief structure. In this way we are perceiving reality.

Now our external reality can conform to our individual belief structure because every atom in creation is conscious, has its own intelligence and is connected to the supreme intelligence, which gives direction. What we are perceiving as reality is a multi-sensual holographic image that corresponds to our mental concepts. This is all being controlled by the supreme Lord, through his interactions with the atomic intelligence through a cosmic code and through time.

Now we all seem to be frequenting, or occupying, the same universe. We are all interacting with one another, and we all seem to be perceiving the same world. We are seeing the same shapes and colors, etc. This is because the objects of the world all have certain characteristics of energy and electromagnetic fields that form specific colors and shapes, etc. More specifically, these energies translate into specific colors and shapes. Our human bodies have been genetically programmed to experience these colors and shapes etc. in the same specific fashion as everyone else.

Our cultural conditioning also programs our mind and senses to interpret the information in a specific format. We, as individuals in modern society, all have similar belief structures of the forms of external reality, so we will view our external world in a similar fashion. Because we have many similarities of beliefs, we can all interact together and perceive the external world in a similar fashion. But what if we took a "primitive" tribesman from the Amazon jungle, who has a different concept, or belief system, of reality. His perceptions may have many similarities, such as shape and color, but there would also be many differences.

There are still many dissimilarities between each individual, especially in one's internal conditioning. Our internal realities are very

PERCEPTIONS OF REALITY

different from each other. For example, there are different philosophies, religions, ideals, values, beliefs etc. that each person possesses that make each person very unique. Our internal realities very much affect our external realities. Not only in the way we spoke about earlier (by attracting certain energies towards us) but also in how the external world interacts with us in other ways.

So we are all occupying the same universe, but simultaneously, each of us is occupying his or her own private universe that is separate from all others. We are connected, yet simultaneously we are divided. In our personal divided universe, all of the material elements are interacting with us in accordance to our belief structures. This is happening in a way that is affecting other peoples individual universes, but usually only in conformity with their own belief structures.

This principle is manifest in our everyday lives by the fact that we are all occupying the same external world, but each individual person perceives him or herself as the center of his or her world, and everybody and everything else is the peripheral. We are simultaneously occupying a collective and an individual universe.

By changing our conditioning and belief structure, we change our perspective, which then changes our perceptions. The external reality will then conform to those perceptions. Our brain will then interpret the external world in a different way. The energies of the external world will also conform to our new belief structure. We will still be occupying the same external universe as everyone else, but that external universe will be perceived differently and will interact with us in a different fashion.

For example, the shape shifters of many cultures have been able to change their perceptions of reality, so that the reality acts in a different way. They perceive the world as the dream time, or a multi-sensual holographic projection. They are able to enter into the higher di-

PERCEPTIONS OF REALITY

mensions of consciousness that are not perceptible to our "normal" mental states. From these higher perspectives they are able to change the states of the various energies and the frequencies of the electromagnetic energy fields and restructure them. By their restructuring process in these higher dimensions of consciousness, they are able to change their physical reality. They are able to break down the electromagnetic fields and rebuild them in different forms. The physical projection changes form to conform with their perceptions. By this process they are able to change the laws of physical space.

They are still participating in the collective external environment, but their internal consciousness is occupying a different level. Their perspective is not the same as ours. Their consciousness is acting from a much higher perspective, which allows them to live according to a different set of universal laws that don't conform to ours, yet they are still interacting with the same external world that we live in.

In the same way, each time we are able to shift our consciousness to a higher perspective, then the external world will shift to match our new perception of reality. We will be able to magnetize different energies to us and create a different outcome of events. The more that we are able to let go of our "normal" perspective of consciousness and reach a higher perspective, the more we will be able to transform our external reality. This occurs while we are still simultaneously inhabiting the same external world of the rest of the population.

Sometimes persons of a higher consciousness may come into our lives, and their higher reality bleeds into our lives. Because of this phenomenon, we can experience what is known as miracles. They are glimpses of another reality; one that does not conform to our belief structures. These are hints that tell us that there is something beyond our perceptions of reality.

PERCEPTIONS OF REALITY

The Power of Thought and Emotion

Every thought has power. When the thought is expressed, it increases in power. We express from the chakra center of the throat, which is the center of expression. The two primary organs of expression are the voice and the hands. I lived in Italy for many years, and as everyone knows, Italians speak as much with their hands as they do with their voice. I consider the Italians as the experts of expression.

When we speak our thoughts, we give them power. When we express our thoughts with the voice combined with hand movements, the power of the expression becomes more powerful. When we write our thoughts with our hands, it gives them even more power.

Now if each thought has a potential, and if we express the thoughts with the voice and hands it creates more potential, then we need to become aware of our thoughts and the expression of them. Each thought gives direction to our intention. Our intention moves our consciousness into a particular direction.

If our thoughts are of a negative nature, such as failure, need, fear, anger, etc., then our intention and consciousness are directed in that direction. When this happens, it gives energy to the universe to magnetize energies that resonate with those thoughts. For example, if we desire prosperity in our lives, and we constantly think of the lack of prosperity in our lives, then the potential of those thoughts magnetizes to us the very thing that we are trying to avoid. On the other hand, if we think positive thoughts of prosperity, then prosperity will be attracted towards us.

Emotions are even more powerful than thoughts. The combination of thought and emotion creates feelings, which are even more powerful. Feelings are the sensation of emotion combined with the direction of your thought in regards to your perception of your present

PERCEPTIONS OF REALITY

experience. Our perception, which is dependent upon our perspective, dictates how we will feel about any given situation. Our perspective is affected by our previous conditioning, which creates a preconceived judgment, or belief structure.

Therefore, depending upon our conditioning, we will perceive each situation in a certain way that creates certain thoughts, emotions and feelings. If we have a pattern of viewing failure in our lives, then each time we are presented with an opportunity, we will see the possibility of failure, which in turn creates thoughts, feelings and emotions of failure. These, in turn, will magnetize events that resonate with these thoughts, feelings and emotions. By this process, our belief that we are failures will be confirmed.

The importance of our thoughts cannot be overemphasized. But from where do thoughts come from? They come from our minds as a result of our associations with material energy. Depending on our associations, different thoughts appear in our minds. This is why advertising is so affective. We see programs and commercials on television, we speak to people, read, socialize, and so many other activities. All of these experiences give rise to thoughts concerning those experiences. Our memories are filled with information that give rise to thought. Some thoughts seem to come from nowhere, but if analyzed properly, we can see that the origin is from association either from the past or present. Sometimes they can be transferred from other persons in our association. For example, if I think about apple pie, and someone brings me one without my asking, then that was a transference of thought.

We, as individuals, have the power to control our thoughts to some degree. As thoughts appear in our minds, we have the ability to let them pass out or dwell on them. Thoughts that pass out quickly, if not coupled with emotion, have very little potency. But thoughts that we dwell upon have much more potency. If we dwell upon them long

PERCEPTIONS OF REALITY

enough, they will also create emotions and feelings that correlate to the thought. These will then cause pressure towards expression. If we are negatively conditioned by our experiences, we will express our thoughts and emotions by complaining, arguing, criticizing, etc. By these expressions, we then attract the appropriate energies that resonate to the expression.

Some emotions are very powerful, such as fear, and these emotions, and the thoughts that accompany them, cannot be pushed away. If we try to think them away, we are actually giving them more energy. By trying to think away something that we don't want in life, in actuality we are placing a tremendous amount of energy and intention onto that which we are trying to avoid. This in turn will magnetize the situation to us.

So the best way to release thoughts and emotions that we don't want to experience is not to think about them at all. Instead, we should replace the thoughts and emotions with the opposite, or that which we want to occur. Put your attention towards positive thoughts and actions to accomplish your goal.

Just about everyone has some past conditioning that creates negative thoughts and emotions that hinder one's development. These past conditionings affect our perceptions to such an extent, that they create a pathway for our lives to follow. Our perceptions direct the energy of consciousness into specific directions that we will follow.

By seeing the perfection of the world and the positive affects of our painful experiences, it releases the charge that is related to the experience. When this happens, our conditioning changes, which then changes our perspective, which in turn changes our perception. When the perception is changed, then the direction of our intention changes, as well of the direction in our life. We then create new pathways for our lives to follow.

PERCEPTIONS OF REALITY

The Power of Gratitude

As we release the negative emotions concerning our experiences, we become free of their effects. We have been discussing how to do this in a simple formula. Every time we experience a painful situation, we must look for the positive effects of the experience that improved our life. This could be lessons learned, new opportunities, etc. When the negative charge is released, there is something else that takes its place, and that is gratitude.

Gratitude is a very powerful emotion that can change our lives. By giving thanks and feeling thankful, it opens a doorway. This doorway allows abundance to enter our lives. It puts our attention to the positive and puts out a message to the universe that we are open to receive. When we are grateful, the universe responds by giving more in return. If we look at our lives and acknowledge the things that we are thankful for, we open this door of abundance that gives us more of that which we are thankful for.

For example, if we find ourselves in a situation in life that isn't making us happy, if we put our attention on the things that don't make us happy, it compounds the problem. If, instead, we feel gratitude for the positive aspects of the situation, then it gives us and the universe the power to change the situation.

Let's say you don't like your house and you want to move. If you concentrate your attention and energy on what you don't like about your house, it just makes it worse. It may become so bad that eventually you move, but you've then left the situation with a bad attitude.

All of the negative feelings that have accumulated from your attitude will create magnetic forces that will attract similar situations. Because of this, you will be attracted to a new house that will begin manifesting new problems that you will again notice. This will create the feeling of having to move again. I am speaking of this from expe-

PERCEPTIONS OF REALITY

rience. In the past I have moved from city to city, and country to country for years trying to avoid this problem that was inside me all along. Wherever you go, you take yourself with you.

If instead we see the good points of our house, how it has given us shelter, maybe the rent was cheap, or it was close to work, or had a nice view, etc., then we can feel gratitude, which in turn, opens a doorway that allows for new possibilities. Then, if we do move, we won't be carrying with us the negative thoughts, feelings and emotions associated with the old house. That way, when we move, we won't be facing the same problems again. We will be content.

The difference that created these two separate outcomes was in our perception of the situation. The perception created a specific attitude, or state of mind, that attracted to it resonating energies that created the specific outcome.

If you could feel appreciation and gratitude for everything that has happened in your life, you could make a quantum leap in consciousness. Looking back on your life and acknowledging gratitude for the many good things that have happened in life creates a very powerful energy that can alter your life and bring you to a higher level of perspective. When you achieve that higher consciousness, it magnetizes certain energies to heal your body, mind and soul. It brings abundance and joy and releases the negative emotions that hold you back in life.

If you can look back at all of the situations that you perceived as negative and painful and saw the benefits and lessons that those situations brought you, you would be able to become free of the negative emotions and energies that are connected to those situations. When this happens, you will become free from the conditioning that those situations created. When you become free of these negative influences, you will begin to feel gratitude for those situations in your life, and a new perception of life will appear in its place. This is the

PERCEPTIONS OF REALITY

most healing power to change your life. You will notice how the world will reciprocate by magnetizing positive energies into your life; how difficult situations will shift to create new positive outcomes.

Imagine if everyday you chose one painful situation in your life and healed it by seeing the positive benefits and lessons those situations brought you. Where do you think you would be in one month? Where would you be in one year? Every night before you go to rest, reflect upon your day and appreciate everything that happened to you. If there was a seemingly negative situation, see how that situation benefitted you. What lessons did you learn?

There is nothing that happens to us that is not meant for our growth and evolution of consciousness, and all of these events are being orchestrated by the supreme Lord. If you refuse to acknowledge the benefits and lessons that seemingly painful situations bring, then you cannot learn the lessons involved in those situations. What will happen instead is that you will harbor resentment, anger and bitterness, and the lessons will appear to you in other situations. This will continue until you understand the lessons and feel gratitude for them. As soon as you heal a situation by seeing the positive benefits and feeling gratitude, you can release the negative emotions and conditioning that it produced. You will become free from the bondage that it produced, and you will no longer have to experience that lesson. If you were to adopt this simple principle in your life, I can assure you that you will make a quantum leap in consciousness that will change your life forever. I have never found a more powerful principle in life.

There are different potencies of gratitude. If we think of gratitude, it creates some energy that will create some effect. If we feel gratitude also in our hearts, then the potency is magnified tremendously. If we express the gratitude verbally, then it is again increased and manifests the results more quickly. If we write the thanks with our hands, then it is again increased.

PERCEPTIONS OF REALITY

When we feel gratitude it opens our heart. Our soul is situated in our heart. God is also situated in our heart. Gratitude then opens the doorway to our heart, which opens the doorway to our soul and to God. This occurs because the vibration of gratitude resonates with the vibration of the heart. It is like a key that unlocks the potential of our soul and God. The feeling of gratitude in the heart creates the feeling of love. This in turn creates a resonating frequency that affects our physical body and our mind. It creates a healing affect on our body and mind and also on our consciousness.

It has been scientifically proven that when we feel negative emotions such as fear or anger, the body becomes weaker. Even the muscles lose their strength. If we feel positive emotions, such as love, compassion or gratitude, the body becomes stronger.

The emotional body is also affected by gratitude. It creates a resonating frequency that calms the emotions and synchronizes them to the vibration of the heart. The emotions are the most magnetic force in attracting different energies and events in our lives. By calming the emotions with love and gratitude, it allows the magnetic attraction of positive events and experiences to manifest in our lives.

There are other aspects of our being that are affected by gratitude. It creates a resonating energy field that heals and energizes all of the chakra centers, which in turn heal and energize all of the aspects of ourselves that are connected to those chakra centers.

The feeling of gratitude, when it enters our heart, puts us in closer touch to our soul and to God. When this happens, something else happens. It opens the doorway to the abstract mind. This is the part of the mind that connects the right and left hemispheres of the brain; the rational, logical half of the mind and the creative, intuitive half of the mind. It also connects the male and female aspects of ourselves.

This is the point of balance between polar opposites. This point of balance creates an incredible affect on the consciousness. In this bal-

PERCEPTIONS OF REALITY

anced point of awareness, a new and different form of thinking takes place. This is the seat of genius. In this seat of awareness one can see the larger picture; the connections and relationships of things; new solutions to problems; different viewpoints to situations. It creates a new and elevated point of perspective of which to perceive the reality.

It is the gratitude that opens the heart, fills it with love, and connects you with your soul and God. This connection, in turn, opens a doorway in the mind that creates a different form of awareness. It is like if a light went on in your head. In effect this is true, because what happens is the crown chakra opens and spiritual light flows in and inundates the mind.

When the abstract mind is opened, another phenomenon takes place. This is the descent of inspiration and revelation. Inspirations for new inventions or new solutions come forth. When the abstract mind opens, it creates a connection directly to the heart, where the soul and God are situated. When this happens, God reveals certain divine truths through revelation. These revelations are doorways into the spiritual realms, where there are no limits of time and space. In this state of awareness one becomes free from the confines of normal mental activities and becomes aware of a new form of mental function.

Because there is a direct connection between the abstract mind and the soul, the revelation comes from God, through the soul and into the abstract mind, where it grows. The balanced abstract mind, with its higher state of mental function, then contemplates the revelation.

There is another phenomenon that takes place when we access the abstract mind. Not only can we perceive a larger picture of reality, but also a deeper picture. We can observe the causes behind seemingly random events and circumstances. We can see what's behind the apparent reality - the deeper meanings of things. We can also begin to distinguish the truth from the non truth. Because our perspective is

PERCEPTIONS OF REALITY

closer to those of the prophets and sages, we can also begin to understand their revelations. We can understand their metaphors, and their analogies. Their explanations of the absolute become more accessible, and when we read the holy scriptures, we can comprehend the true meanings. We will also be able to distinguish which parts of the scriptures are true, which ones have been fabricated, and which ones have been corrupted. We will be able, once and for all, to understand the three basic questions of life; "Who am I?" "From where have I come?" and "What is this place?"

From this information we can see the amazing power of gratitude. Not only does it create positive situations in our life by magnetizing abundance and other positive energies, but it also heals our body and mind. It opens the doorway to the heart; which opens the doorway to the soul and God; which then opens the doorway to the abstract mind; the abstract mind then opens the doorway to inspiration and revelation; which then opens the doorway to the spiritual sky. Therefore, gratitude is the key that opens the doorways to the heavens.

About the Author

Gregory Calise has experienced many variations of life in his search for truth. He has spent fifteen years living overseas in six countries and has traveled through twenty-five countries. He has worked in a variety of occupations, ranging from corporate, personnel and sales management to architecture, ceramics, art, cooking and teaching yoga.

Gregory has researched most religious doctrines, and he has practiced Christianity, Tibetan and Zen Bhuddism, Vedanta, Vaishnavism, Shamanism, and New Age philosophies. He has lived in Monasteries, gone on pilgrimages, lectured extensively on yoga and lived in the secular community. By experiencing the many paths of life and over thirty years of practicing meditation, contemplation, observation, and devotion, he has received several revelations and has been able to shift his perspective to a higher state of consciousness. From this higher perspective of consciousness the larger picture of reality is perceived, where one can discern the truth from the distortions.

ISBN 1553956613